COMPUTER MONOGRAPHS

General Editor: Stanley Gill, M.A., Ph.D., *Professor of Computing Science, Imperial College, London*
Associate Editor: J. J. Florentin, Ph.D., *Imperial College, London*

8

COMPILING TECHNIQUES

COMPILING TECHNIQUES

F.R.A. HOPGOOD
Atlas Computer Laboratory, Science Research Council

MACDONALD: LONDON
AND
AMERICAN ELSEVIER INC.: NEW YORK

First published in 1969
Second impression 1969
Third impression 1970
Fourth impression 1970

Sole distributors for the United States and Dependencies
American Elsevier Publishing Company, Inc.
52 Vanderbilt Avenue
New York, N.Y. 10017

Sole Distributors for the British Isles and Commonwealth
Macdonald & Co. (Publishers) Ltd
P.O. Box 2 L.G.
49–50 Poland Street
London W.1

All remaining areas
Elsevier Publishing Company
P.O. Box 211
Jan van Galenstraat 335
Amsterdam
The Netherlands

British SBN 356 02474 1
American SBN 444 19769 9
Library of Congress Catalog Card No. 69 12573

PRINTED AND BOUND IN ENGLAND BY
HAZELL WATSON AND VINEY LTD
AYLESBURY, BUCKS

ACKNOWLEDGMENT

Sections of this book originated as Lecture Notes for a Summer School for Systems Programmers organised by the Ministry of Technology's Advanced Computer Techniques Project in June 1966. I would like to thank Her Majesty's Stationery Office for permission to use this material.

CONTENTS

1

INTRODUCTION

1.1 Definition of a compiler

The name *compiler* has been given to a computer program which will accept as data a program in a problem-oriented language, such as Algol or Fortran, and produce as output a computer-oriented code which, after possibly some further processing by an *assembler* or *loader*, will be capable of being obeyed by a computer and produce results equivalent to those defined by the program in the problem-oriented language. This definition is rather vague and has to be as the word *compiler* is used for rather a wide range of computer programs with very different characteristics.

In this book, the problem-oriented language to be compiled will be assumed to be as machine independent and as complex as a language like Fortran or Algol. Most examples will be drawn from one or other of these languages. There is a bias towards scientific languages of this type in the techniques to be described although, of course, many of the techniques will be applicable in general. The output from the compiler will be defined in machine orders for a hypothetical computer which will be similar to most of the single accumulator computers in use today.

1.2 The structure of a compiler

A compiler can be broken down into several distinct sections, each of which performs a specific task. Each of these sections can be thought of as having specific input data and output, so that each section can be thought of as a sub-program. On small computers, where the size of program that can be fitted into the main store is severely limited, it is usual to split the compiler into these sub-programs and have one sub-program complete its task for the whole program before the next is called. If, however, the complete compiler can be fitted easily into the main store, then it is often the case that the sub-programs are entered cyclically so that one part of the input program is nearly completely compiled before the next part of the input program is examined. Although these two methods will require completely different control structures, the techniques used will not be very different.

1

The program in the problem-oriented language is often punched on paper tape or cards, using some external piece of equipment, and presented to the computer to be input by one of the readers on the computer. Alternatively, parts of the program may reside within the computer in previously defined files. In most systems there are several ways in which the program can be presented. Consequently, it is usual to have an initial section to the compiler whose purpose is to provide an interface between the outside world and the rest of the compiler. The aim is that the same program presented to the compiler in several different ways will be identical as far as the remainder of the compiler is concerned, once it has passed through this initial phase. Most programming languages allow a certain amount of redundancy in the preparation of the program. For example, spaces can often be inserted to aid readability, and new lines inserted as desired. These redundancies are also removed by this initial phase which is usually described as *lexical analysis*.

When lexical analysis has been completed it is necessary to recognise the individual statements that make up the program and, if a statement is complex, to break it down into its simpler parts. In general, programming languages are defined so that this *syntax analysis* can be done without knowing the meaning of the statement. This phase of the compiler will verify that the program is grammatically correct and the output will exhibit the structure of the program found by this analysis.

Each statement of the program must now be examined and the equivalent computer code generated. For many statements this *code generation* will be straightforward. Certain statement types can always have a fixed sequence of code generated with only a few fields which change depending on the exact form of this statement type in the program. The fixed sequence of code, which is stored away ready for use, is called a *skeleton*.

If it is important to use as little storage as possible or, alternatively, to make the program run as fast as possible, then it is necessary to *optimise* the simple code generation described above. More analysis will be required on individual statements and any interaction between neighbouring statements must be discovered. For scientific languages it is important that the code generation for arithmetic expressions is efficient as these statements will be a large proportion of the total code obeyed in any program.

1.3 A brief history

The first compilers for higher level languages were produced in the period 1956 to 1958. The most important of these was the Fortran compiler for the IBM 704. The original compiler took eighteen man-years to write and, in some areas, used techniques as sophisticated as any in use today. As the only input medium was punched cards and the Fortran language made statement recognition simple, no special techniques arose for the lexical and syntax analysis parts of the compiler. However, the IBM 704 had only three index registers and, as one of the design aims was to produce code as efficient as that produced by hand, much effort was put into algorithms for index register allocation and optimisation of the code produced for arithmetic expressions. Two papers describing this work are Sheridan (1959) and Backus *et al.* (1957).

A large number of different algorithms for the syntactic and semantic analysis of arithmetic expressions was produced in the period before 1960. These included many methods of the precedence type together with more unusual algorithms. Algorithms were defined, some of which parsed from right to left while others continually changed direction as the statement was scanned. A history of these early methods is given by Randell and Russell (1964).

The 1960 Algol report was the first widely accepted language definition which had the syntax rigorously defined. This together with the BNF notation [Naur *et al.*, (1960)] used in the definition encouraged research into syntax analysis and related subjects. This has continued until the present day, and the syntax analysis phase is the one area where the techniques used are well understood and the relative merits of different techniques estimated.

The acceptance of Algol as an international standard without any defined hardware representation has led to more effort being put into lexical analysis in recent years. In Great Britain, for example there are over ten different external representations of Algol available and work in this area has had to be done to aid program interchange.

Many of the early papers on compiling techniques have been brought together by Rosen (1967).

2

DATA STRUCTURES

2.1 Introduction

Before describing the various parts which comprise a compiler, it is necessary to consider the *abstract data structures* which will be used by the compiler and also how these abstract structures are implemented using particular storage structures. The compilation process can be thought of as taking some input data structure and transforming it to produce an output data structure which in some sense is equivalent to but more desirable than the input form. The input data is often called the *source program* and the output the *object code*. One of the simplest forms the compilation process can take is to have the input data structure coming from a peripheral device (such as a card reader), and the compiler producing as output a machine code program in the store of the computer ready for execution. In most compilers, before the output form is arrived at, the input data structure may well be transformed into several internal data structures. The compiler itself may require to store additional information or alternatively be *driven* by information stored internally. Finally, the data structures defined in the source program in the specific programming language must be mapped into some storage structure on the background computer that is to execute the program. The problems which need to be resolved when designing a compiler are ones such as finding the most transparent abstract data structure to use at each stage and also the most efficient internal storage structure into which to map the abstract data structure.

2.2 Abstract data structures

A data structure is defined as a set of rules and constraints which show the relationships that exist between individual pieces of data. The structure says nothing about the individual pieces of data which may occur. It may require them to *hold* the structure in some sense, but any information contained in the data items is independent of the structure. The term *item* used here will denote a piece of an abstract data structure. The item itself may be another data structure so that a hierarchical set of data structures is built up.

4

2.2.1 *String*

A *string* is an ordered set of items. The string may either be of variable length or fixed. Each item only has knowledge of its neighbours so that accessing a particular item must be done by a sequential search starting from one of the ends of a string. Examples of operations defined on a string are:

    (a) concatenation of two strings
    (b) comparison of two strings item per item
    (c) breaking strings into several parts.

2.2.2 *Array*

An *array* A is a set of items which are so arranged that an ordered set of integers uniquely defines the position of each item of the array and provides a method of accessing each item directly. Using the notation of Algol, an item of the array A could be written $A[j_1, j_2, j_3, \ldots, j_n]$. If the ordered set of integers has length n, then the array is called *n-dimensional*. The individual integers in the ordered set are called *subscripts*. Each subscript may have its range defined in any way, and it could consist of several disjoint sub-ranges.

A particular subset of arrays, which is used in both compilers and programming languages, is the set of *rectangular arrays*. A rectangular array has the range of each of its subscripts constant and contiguous. For example, the Algol declaration

$$\textbf{array } A[1{:}10, 0{:}5, 3{:}7];$$

defines a three-dimensional array with its subscripts having ranges 10, 6, and 5, respectively. A typical element would be $A[3, 4, 5]$.

2.2.3 *Queues and stacks*

Queues and *stacks* are dynamically changing data structures. At any time, the queue or stack contains an ordered set of items. In the case of a queue, if an item is added, it is placed at the end of the ordered set. Items can only be accessed or removed from the front of the ordered set defining the queue. The first item added to the queue is the only one accessible and must be the first removed. For a stack, items are similarly added to the end of the ordered set. The difference is that the accessing or removal of items from the ordered set is from the end of the set. The last item added is the only one accessible and is the first to be removed. The items may well be of variable length and contain the length defined within the item.

2.2.4 *Tables*

A *table* consists of a set of items, and associated with each item is a unique name, or *key*. In general, each item will consist of its key, together with some information associated with the key. An item can be added to the table by presenting its key together with the associated information. Items are accessed by presenting the key to the table.

2.2.5 Trees

A *tree* is a structure consisting of a set of *nodes*. Each node (or item) has the property that, apart from information that it may carry, it also contains pointers to lower-level nodes. At the lowest level of the tree, the nodes point to *leaves* which consist of data structures external to the tree. The idea of level comes from the fact that each tree must have one top-most node which has no pointers to it from other nodes (this is often called the *root* of the tree) and also no node can point to a node previously defined. This latter condition ensures that each node has a unique path to it from the root. Nodes on level 1 are those pointed at by the root; nodes on level 2 are pointed at from nodes on level 1, and so on.

Fig. 2.1 diagrammatically shows a *binary* tree (each node points to exactly two lower nodes) representing $A*B + C*D$. The letters A, B, C, D denote the leaves and the ringed quantities represent the information associated with the node. It is conventional to represent the tree with the root at the top and leaves at the bottom unlike most natural trees. The * is used to represent multiplication.

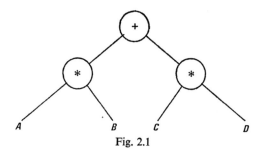

Fig. 2.1

2.2.6 Directed graphs

A *directed graph* is similar to a tree except that the nodes may point to nodes *higher up* the structure. Therefore, a node may have more than one node pointing to it. As it is now no longer obvious which direction the line joining two nodes is pointing; it is usual to mark at least the upward pointing lines in a diagram. The relaxation of the rules for trees now means that it is possible to have a path from a node back to itself. This is commonly called a *loop*. A particular sub-class of directed graphs is the set of *loop-free* directed graphs. This does not coincide with the definition of a tree, however, as it is still allowable for two nodes to point to the same node which is not

6

allowed in the case of trees. For example, the Algol compound statement:

> **begin**
> $a := b := c := 2$;
> first: **if** $a > b$ **then** $z := 4$ **else** $c := 1$;
>   **if** $z > 3$ **then goto** next;
> $b := 1$;
>   **goto** first;
> next: $z := 1$;
> **end**

could be represented by the directed graph given in Fig. 2.2.

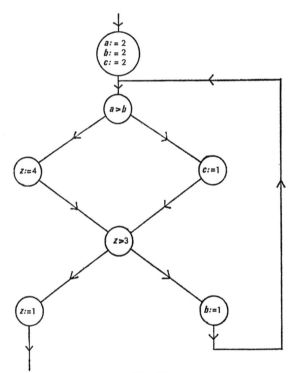

Fig. 2.2

2.3 Internal storage structures

Most computers tend to have a memory consisting of a set of ordered words, and this is the only available storage structure that the computer itself has. In general, by the use of programs and subroutines, higher level storage structures are superimposed upon the basic structure of the computer, and to the user of the subroutines,

7

the computer itself appears to have this structure. A fairly well defined set of such *internal storage structures* have been used and, although they are usually designed so as to be equivalent to an abstract storage structure or at least a structure into which the abstract structure can be easily mapped, they still tend to be influenced by the basic structure of the computer memory.

Each internal storage structure will be built up from indivisible (as far as the structure is concerned) pieces of storage called *elements*. These are closely equivalent to the items of the abstract structure. The element may have several fields some of which could be used in defining the structure. An element could consist of a single bit of a computer word but is more likely to be at least an address field in width.

2.3.1 *Vectors*

A *vector* in most computers is the name given to the basic storage structure of the computer. A vector is a set of elements which are physically adjacent in the computer store. A vector is defined by knowing its *base address*, its *element size*, and its *length* (all elements will be assumed to be the same size). Individual elements can be accessed immediately using the base of the vector and the position of the element in the vector. A vector closely corresponds to the abstract data structure, the one-dimensional array, and almost invariably one-dimensional arrays are mapped into vectors. It will be convenient, therefore, to represent a vector of length N with name A by the Algol declaration:

array $A[1:N]$

and individual elements will be called $A[i]$ for $i = 1$ to N.

2.3.2 *Lists*

A *list* is a set of elements where each element consists of two fields. The second field contains a pointer to the next element in the list. The first field contains a pointer to the information defined by this element. This could be another list or some external data structure. An external data structure will be called an *atom*, and will be assumed to be indivisible as far as operations on the list are concerned. For example, a string of characters $A\ B\ C$ could be represented pictorially as a list by Fig. 2.3.

A list as a whole is accessed by a pointer P, to the first element of the list. The last element of the list either contains a special entry written as $\emptyset$ to denote a null pointer in the second field or alternatively contains a pointer to the initial element of the list, in which case the list is called *circular*.

An actual implementation will have the list element consisting of sufficient bits to define two computer addresses. On some computers

8

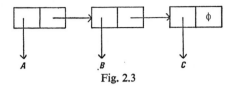

Fig. 2.3

this can be done by using one computer word; on others two words are required. It is important to note that there is no necessity for neighbouring elements to be consecutive in the computer store, and, in fact, they may well be scattered through the computer store. A full description of the operations usually associated with lists can be found in the companion Monograph by J. M. Foster entitled 'List Processing'.

A list is the simplest form in which the sequential storage of a computer can be used in a more flexible manner.

2.3.3 Plexes

Although the lists defined above are capable of representing the more complex abstract data structures such as trees and directed graphs, quite often they will be inefficient and also opaque. For example, the tree in Fig. 2.1 might well be represented as a list by the structure shown in Fig. 2.4.

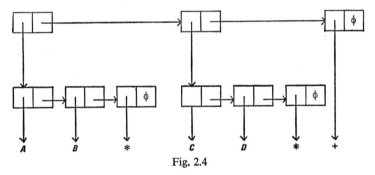

Fig. 2.4

A more efficient and transparent storage structure in this case would be a *plex*. Storage systems similar to the plex have been in wide use for a number of years; a precise definition and theory of plexes and plex programming is due to D. T. Ross of the Massachusetts Institute of Technology. A plex (derived from *plexus* meaning *any complex structure containing an intricate network of interrelated parts*) consists of a set of elements called *beads*, where each element is an N-word vector of computer storage. This N-word block is broken down into a set of fields containing information or alternatively pointers to other beads. With each type of plex is assumed a *format* which defines what the individual fields represent.

9

The format is assumed to be external to the set of beads defining the plex. This can be thought of, therefore, as an extension of the two-word list element to an *n*-word element where fields may contain information as well as pointers. The plex processing system of D. T. Ross closely associates with each plex a set of algorithms which refer to and change the information contained in the plex. In most conventionally produced compilers this association is not usually very precise, although the plex as a storage structure is frequently used. The arithmetic expression shown as a list structure in Fig. 2.4 is shown as a plex in Fig. 2.5. In this example two types of beads are defined; the four word bead for the nodes where the format is denoted by the field N, and the two-word bead where T denotes a leaf. The plex is a fairly natural structure for representing trees and directed graphs in a computer.

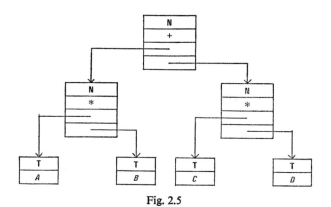

Fig. 2.5

3

DATA STRUCTURE MAPPINGS

This chapter is intended to give some examples of the ways in which the abstract data structures, defined in Chapter 2, are mapped on to internal data structures.

3.1 Stacks and queues

The conventional method of representing a stack in a computer is by a vector. The base of the stack is usually the first position in the vector. A pointer, P, is set to point to the top-most element of the stack. The length of the vector is usually set to the maximum length of the stack that is expected. Insertion of an item consists of incrementing the pointer P and inserting in the address pointed to by P.

A queue, however, is not easily represented as a vector, so it is usually represented by a list. The reason being that, if it was represented as a vector, each time an item was removed from the queue, it would either be necessary to move the elements down the vector to fill up the gap made at the base or alternatively the set of elements in the queue would gradually move down the vector. When represented as a circular list with the *pointer to the list* pointing at the last item added, both adding and removing items from the queue is simple. It can easily be seen that these operations can be achieved without doing a complete search of the list which would be necessary for adding items if the pointer was to the first item of the list.

3.2 Strings

Strings are most usually stored as a vector. Whether or not more than one item of the string is stored in a single computer word depends to a large extent on the operations available in the computer's order code and the operations required upon the string. If it is necessary to do operations on the string, such as breaking the string into two parts or matching two strings, then it is often more reasonable to store the string as a list. If the string can have variable length and matching is required, then it is often useful to keep a count of the number of elements in the string in the initial element.

3.3 Trees and directed graphs

These, in general, require an arbitrary number of pointers from each node and, although it is possible to represent them by list structures, it is more usual to use a plex of some kind. In the case of arithmetic expressions, for example, most operators are binary and the structure shown in Fig. 2.5 would be a reasonable one to use.

In some cases it is necessary to find parts of the tree or graph with the same pattern. In an arithmetic expression, for example, it might be desirable to find common sub-expressions. In this case the nodes of the tree could be stored in a table. The information at the node and the nodes pointed to by this node could define the key. The information part of the table could be used to carry any additional pointers or information required.

3.4 Arrays

Arrays are almost invariably mapped into vectors in the computer store. In the case of arrays which are sparsely filled, that is have only a few non-empty entries, it is sometimes useful to store arrays as a table of the non-empty entries. However, this occurs infrequently and only vector storage will be discussed here.

Representing the vector by **array** $A[1:N]$ then an array defined as:

$$\textbf{array } B[i:j]$$

would normally be mapped such that:

$$B[k] \text{ is mapped into } A[k - i + 1]$$

Similarly, an n-dimensional rectangular array will be mapped into a vector. This is usually done in one of two ways. Either the first subscript is allowed to vary most quickly or alternatively the last. This is best illustrated with an example. The array defined as:

$$\textbf{array } B[1:2, 3:5]$$

would have its items stored in the vector in the order

$$B[1, 3], B[2, 3], B[1, 4], B[2, 4], B[1, 5], B[2, 5] \quad \text{or}$$
$$B[1, 3], B[1, 4], B[1, 5], B[2, 3], B[2, 4], B[2, 5]$$

Given the declaration:

$$\textbf{array } B[i_1:k_1, i_2:k_2, \ldots, i_n:k_n]$$

then the item $B[j_1, j_2, \ldots, j_n]$ could be mapped into the vector in position:

$$A\left[1 + \sum_{m=1}^{n} (j_m - i_m)D_m \right]$$

where $D_1 = 1$ and $D_m = (k_{m-1} - i_{m-1} + 1)D_{m-1}$

3.4.1 *Array accessing using dope vectors*

So far a description of how the array is stored has been given. It is now necessary to describe the way in which an individual item of the array is accessed. The simplest approach adopted is to allow just sufficient space for the array item in the vector and, whenever an item of the array is required, to access it by calculating

$$\sum_{m=1}^{n}(j_m - i_m)D_m$$

However, both D_m and i_m depend only on the array definition and not on the individual item accessed. For efficiency, therefore, the quantity $\sum_{m=1}^{n} i_m D_m$ and the individual D_m values could be stored to avoid recalculation. They could be stored with the array itself, although it is more usual to use a separate vector called the *dope vector*. Two arrays with the same parameters could then, to a large extent, use the same dope vector.

It is possible that a request for an array item is made with either too many or too few subscripts. Also, individual subscripts must be within the declared range. To aid in checking such illegal requests it is usual to store the dimensionality and upper and lower bounds of each subscript in the dope vector.

For example, the declaration for B given as an example might produce two pointers associated with B. The first would point to the vector containing the array items; the second to a dope vector containing:

(1) Number of dimensions
(2) Lower and upper bounds for each subscript
(3) Number of items in array
(4) The D_m for $m = 1$ to n
(5) $\sum_{m=1}^{n} i_m D_m$

Two different arrays sharing the same storage could be defined by having the first pointer pointing to the same vector. Two arrays having the same shape and size could use the same dope vector by having the second pointers the same.

3.4.2 *Array accessing by Iliffe vectors*

A second method of accessing, due to Iliffe, is frequently used. This requires more space but will give faster access for individual items. Stored with each array is a set of pointers. For example, the array defined as:

$$B[4:6, -2:1, 0:1]$$

would be stored by a structure shown in Fig. 3.1. Using the notation (B + 5) to mean *the contents of the address B + 5* then the item $B[i, j, k]$ is accessed by:

$$(((C) + i) + j) + k$$

The contents of location C are taken, i is added to this, and the contents of this address give a pointer to the next level down, and so on.

It is important to note that accessing an array item does not now require any multiplications. However, in the example one 3-vector and three 4-vectors are required as well as the array vector itself; that is, instead of 24 elements, 39 elements are required. The method is most economical when the ranges of the subscripts are increasing so that the largest range is the last subscript. It is most inefficient when the largest range is the first subscript.

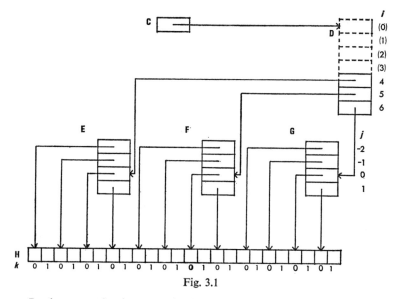

Fig. 3.1

In the example given no check has been made that the subscript given is a legal one. This could be introduced by storing with each element of the Iliffe vector the lower and upper bound of the subscript. For the case of the rectangular array this could be uneconomical. The vectors E, F and G in the example would all have each element with the same lower and upper bounds. It is important to note, however, that these elements could have different subscript bounds, and a much more complex array structure can be accessed by the use of Iliffe vectors.

For example, Fig. 3.2 shows a set of Iliffe vectors for accessing a

14

three dimensional array having only the following items stored in order:

$B[4,-1,-1]$, $B[4,-1,0]$, $B[4,-1,1]$, $B[4,-1,2]$, $B[4,0,0]$,
$B[4,0,1]$, $B[4,0,2]$, $B[4,0,3]$, $B[4,0,4]$, $B[4,0,5]$, $B[4,0,6]$,
$B[5,1,2]$, $B[5,2,2]$, $B[5,2,3]$, $B[5,3,2]$, $B[5,3,3]$, $B[5,3,4]$,
$B[5,3,5]$, $B[6,0,0]$, $B[6,0,1]$, $B[6,0,2]$, $B[6,0,3]$, $B[6,0,4]$,
$B[6,0,5]$

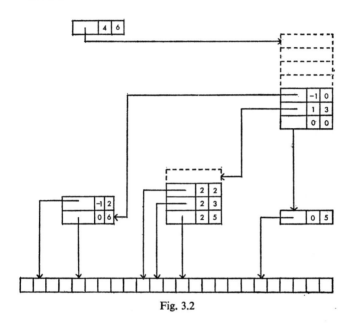

Fig. 3.2

15

4

TABLES

The most usual method of storing a table is in a vector. However, lists and plexes are more usual for certain special types of tables, such as *decision tables*. As stated previously, a table is a storage device for items each having a unique name or key associated with them. The key is given, and on a table access, a pointer to the information associated with the item is returned by the table accessing mechanism. If this information is small in size, then the information itself may be returned. In the case of adding an entry to the table, given the key, the table entry mechanism should return with a pointer to where the information is to be stored. For example, in an English-French dictionary, the English word, for which the French equivalent is required, is the key to the table entry, and the corresponding French word is the information accessed by the key.

In many of the implementations of a table, the insertion and retrieval of information are not based on the key itself but on information dependent on the key. Given a key, k, then a *mapping function* M is defined such that $M(k)$ is the derived information. The function M is used to produce a simpler and more efficient *derived key* for accessing entries. In the example of the English-French dictionary, the book may have a thumb index, and it is then more efficient to use the thumb index to access the section equivalent to the initial letter of the English word and then to find the entry in the section by a search over the remaining letters. In this case the accessing has been divided into two parts with $M_1(k)$ being the initial letter and $M_2(k)$ the remainder of the English word. In most compiler applications the mapping function will produce a numeric (usually integer) result in some range. Such a mapping function will be denoted by $I(k)$.

4.1 Direct access tables

In the English-French dictionary suppose that there are only a limited number of English words which need to be looked up and it so happens that no two English words start with the same letter. In this case if a vector of 26 elements was available and each element was capable of holding the equivalent French word, than all that would be needed is a mapping function $I(k)$ such that for a word

16

k, $I(k)$ is the position in the alphabet of the initial letter of the word k. The $I(k)$th position in the vector would then be set to contain the equivalent French word. Such a table would be called *direct access*. Some properties of direct access tables are:

(1) If the number of English words to be looked up is less than 26 then some elements of the vector are not used and will be wasted.

(2) It is not necessary to store the key k itself as the mapping function is unique.

(3) If, later, an English word with the same initial letter as one already entered is to be added then the method breaks down and a different mapping function must be defined.

This may be defined more precisely. Given a vector A having elements $A[1]$ to $A[n]$ and a mapping function I for a set of keys k_1, k_2 ..., k_m (where $m \leqslant n$) such that $I(k)$ takes a value between 1 and n for all keys and $I(k_i) \neq I(k_j)$ for any i and j, then the accessing is equivalent to an array access and the process can be thought of as mapping the table on to an array.

4.2 Table look-up

The direct access method is only applicable if a mapping function can be found so that the proportion of unused entries is small. If in the dictionary example only five English words were required to be looked-up, then 21 of the 26 storage elements of the vector would be wasted. The *table look-up* is a method which economises on storage at the expense of efficiency. The five words could be stored in consecutive elements of a vector and, assuming that the vector element can contain the French word in another field, then to find the French equivalent of the English word it is necessary to search through the elements in some well defined order comparing the English word that is to be looked-up with the English word in each element. When a match is found, that element contains the equivalent French word. It is important to notice that adding additional entries to the dictionary is simple. These are added at the first empty position in the vector. The vector can either be defined as long as the maximum number of elements ever likely to be added or alternatively a more sophisticated allocation scheme may be arranged. To aid in adding new entries it is usual to reserve the first two positions in the vector for the length of the table and the position of the first empty entry.

4.3 Search length

In comparing the efficiency of the various methods of table access it is necessary to introduce the quantity S, defined as *the length of search* required to find a particular entry in the dictionary. By this is meant the number of dictionary entries that had to be examined before the correct entry was found. In the case of the *direct access table*, $S = 1$ for all entries. For table look-up, the Mth entry has $S = M$.

To get a measure of the efficiency of the accessing method, a second quantity T is introduced which is the average length of search time required to find an entry in the table. In general this will of course depend on the frequency with which entries are accessed. For example, if the first entry in a look-up table is required much more frequently than the remaining entries then the value of T will be approximately 1. If the access frequency in unknown, each entry will be assumed to be accessed the same number of times. This *average length of search* will be denoted by A.

$$A = \frac{1}{n} \sum_{i=1}^{n} S_i$$

for n entries where the search length for the ith entry is S_i. Obviously $A = 1$ for the direct access table and for table look-up with M entries $A = \frac{1}{2}(M + 1)$.

In this case the trade-off for a more efficient storage allocation is a longer average search time. In the case of a table with 39 entries the average length of search for table look-up is $A = 20$. Therefore, unless T is much less than A, this kind of search length is too expensive. More sophisticated methods have, therefore, been adopted to access tables.

4.4 Binary search

Returning to the example of the English-French dictionary, great help is given to the user in finding a particular entry by having the entries in alphabetical order. For any entry required, if the dictionary is opened at any word then it is known whether the required word is before or after this position in the dictionary. A simple algorithm for finding the required entry would, therefore, be to open the dictionary in the middle and see if the word looked at was the required word. If not, then it is known whether the required word is in the first or second half of the dictionary. Suppose the word required was in the first half, then the next step would be to look at the middle entry of the first half. If this was not the required entry then once more it would be known in which half of the first half of the dictionary the required word is contained. The procedure is repeated until the required word is matched. This technique is called *binary search*.

For a table or dictionary of N entries, the length of search S for most entries will be approximately $\log_2 N$ and the average length of search A will not be very much less than $\log_2 N$ as the large number of entries found after approximately $\log_2 N$ entries will predominate. More precisely, this method can be defined as finding a mapping function I which produces a unique set of integers, and then the table entries are ordered depending on the values $I(k)$.

A modification of the standard binary search is to attempt to make a better guess at the position to try at each step rather than try the middle of the table. For example, if the English word in the example was CAT, then it would seem reasonable to try approximately $2/26$ of the way from the front initially. How good a guess is made depends on how much is known about the dictionary. For example, knowing how many words in the English language start with each letter would enable a better initial guess to be made. In a compiler it will quite often be the case that the actual entries will be a non-random subset of entries taken from the complete set of entries about which some general information is known. In this case Peterson (1957) has shown that the average search length A is approximately $\frac{1}{2} \log_2 N$. For a table with 1000 entries the average length of search would be 5 in place of 10 with the straightforward binary search.

The big drawback with this method, which makes it less useful in a compiler, is that adding further entries is not usually a simple process and will require re-ordering of the entries. It is usually used, therefore, for fairly fixed tables where entries are seldom added.

4.5 Hash tables

The most frequently used of the more sophisticated methods of table accessing is the *hash table*. This method first seems to have appeared in some reports by H. P. Luhn and A. D. Lin in 1953 and was used by A. L. Samuel, G. M. Amdahl and E. Boehm in an assembler for the IBM 701 in 1954. The name hash table is usual in the U.S.A. although it frequently goes under the name *computed entry table* in Great Britain. Alternative names for the method that have appeared in the literature are *scatter, randomized* or *key transformation table*.

For a fixed length table, the method usually gives a value for A comparable with the more sophisticated methods while being more flexible than the methods, such as binary search, which require re-ordering. In the methods described so far, the mapping function I has been defined to produce a unique set of integers such that, for any two keys k_1 and k_2, $I(k_1) \neq I(k_2)$. In general, the span of the possible values of $I(k)$ is usually too large to use a direct access table. However, given a table consisting of a vector of length M, it may well be possible to produce a mapping function such that the span of the values of $I(k)$ is 1 to M if the uniqueness condition is dropped. That is, it is possible to have two keys k_1 and k_2 such that $I(k_1) = I(k_2)$.

This table, called a hash table, can be loaded and accessed as though it was a direct access table until a key k_2 is entered where $I(k_1) = I(k_2)$ and k_1 is a key already entered. The k_1 key has been entered in position $I(k_1)$. The problem is where to place the k_2 entry. This situation is called *overflow* and the different sub-methods of the hash class depend on the method used to deal with overflow.

4.5.1 *Open hash*

The *open hash* technique is the method most generally used in compilers. Given a key k, the algorithm for entering or accessing the key in a table of length M is:

(1) Calculate $i = I(k)$.

(2) If the position i in the table is empty or contains the key k in the *name field* of the element then exit.

(3) If not, set $i = i + 1$ (mod M) and go back to step 2.

In this and all methods of the hash type, the key for the entry is stored in a field of the table entry called the *name field*. The search for an entry will always terminate as long as the table is not completely full because of the enforced circularity of step 3.

For example, suppose that in the English-French dictionary it is known that not more than eight words will be required in the dictionary and only words with initial letters A to H will be required. Initially, the table will be assumed empty, and as each word required appears, it is added to the table. The key, that is the English word, is added to the table, together with the French equivalent which is entered in another field of the element. One of the simplest forms that the mapping function I could take would be for $I(k)$ to be the position in the alphabet of the initial letter of the word k. If now the actual words required in order were CAT, DOG, COLD, DAY, HOT HAY, then the table would have been as in Fig. 4.1. The first and second words CAT and DOG are mapped into the third and fourth positions, respectively, and, as they are empty, are inserted there. COLD is mapped into the third entry also, but, as it is not empty, the fourth entry is tried. This is also non-empty, so the fifth entry is tried. This *is* empty and COLD is inserted there. DAY is mapped into the fourth position. This and position 5 are tried, but both are non-empty, so it is inserted in position 6. HOT is mapped into position 8 and entered as it is empty. HAY is also mapped into position 8. This is now occupied so the next entry is tried which, by the circularity, is entry 1. This is empty, therefore, HAY is inserted there.

In the diagram it is assumed that the hash table is organized as a vector with each element having two fields. It is assumed that both the English and French words may be stored in the element of the vector. Quite often this will not be the case. For example, both the English and French words can be of variable length and it would be uneconomical to allow space for the longest possible words. There-fore, it may be necessary to have either or both the key and information fields indirectly addressed. The hash table would then contain pointers to the information which could be stored tightly packed in a separate vector. If either or both the key and information fields vary greatly then this may well be the most efficient storage method.

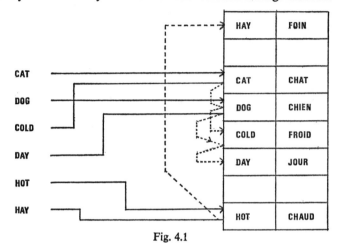

Fig. 4.1

In the example, the two elements mapped into the third position and the two elements mapped into the fourth position have inter-mingled. In order to access DAY the entries looked at include entries mapped into the third position (in this case COLD). The adjective *open* derives from this property that the entries searched from a particular entry position are *open* to elements mapped into other entry positions.

An important result which should always be kept in mind when designing a mapping function is that for *random entries* the average length of scan is minimised if the mapping function maps equal numbers of keys on to the vector positions 1 to M. In general, this may not be possible because of the size of the vector and the size of the set of possible keys. In this case the mapping should be as close to this desired form as possible.

In the example, a cluster of entries has started to appear following the third and fourth positions. This is unavoidable with the open hash technique. However, if the mapping function is badly designed it may be that there is a high correlation between the probabilities of keys appearing that are mapped into neighbouring entries. Care should be taken that this does not occur, for, if it does, much larger clusters than are necessary will be produced, causing the average length of search to be increased. It may be difficult to alter the mapping function I to stop neighbouring entries being correlated

21

without making I very complex. Another approach is to redefine the term neighbour by changing rule (3) of the open hash definition to:

(3) If not, set $i = i + P$ (mod M) and go back to step 2.

The constant 1 has been replaced by P. As long as M and P are co-prime all positions of the vector will still be searched. However, the *nearest neighbours* of position i are now $i + P$, $i + 2P$, etc. This change is equivalent to redefining a more complex mapping function, and all results obtained for $P = 1$ apply for a general P.

In order to simplify the circularity of the table it is usual to have M a power of 2, say 2^R, in which case a simple mask of R bits is sufficient to take the modulus. Also, this usually helps the definition of the mapping function if this is being done at a machine-code level. One inconvenience of a hash table is that, during the debugging stage of writing a compiler, entries will appear fairly randomly throughout the table, which is not very convenient for print-out. It is quite often useful, therefore, to parameterise the routines for accessing the table so that it is easy to change both I and P. In this case, during the debug phase, P could be set to 1, and a mapping function I, when $I(k) = 1$ for all k, could be used. The table is then transformed to a simple table look-up.

It is not easy to determine the average length of search A for an open hash table because of the effect of clustering described earlier. Even assuming that the mapping function maps equally on to all positions and assuming that the keys are taken randomly from the set of all possible keys, then it is not possible to assume that the entries in the table are randomly distributed as clustering appears as soon as a significant number of entries have been made. Let the average search length be defined as $A(\sigma)$ where $\sigma = N/M$, the fraction that the table is filled (sometimes this will be written $A(N,M)$). N is the number of entries so far inserted in the table of length M. Peterson (1957) did a set of nine simulation runs with keys mapped randomly into the range 1 to 500. The results for these are given in Table 4.1. One point worthy of notice is that the values of $A(\sigma)$ are independent of the order in which the N entries were inserted. Any permutation of the order can be broken down into a set of legal permutations involving only two entries. Reversing the order of insertion of just two entries can easily be shown to give the same length of search for the two elements. Schay and Spruth (1962) assumed that, in a cluster, all entries mapped into the ith position appeared before those mapped into the $(i + 1)$th. They were then able to obtain the approximate formula:

$$A(\sigma) = \frac{2 - \sigma}{2 - 2\sigma}$$

This is also tabulated in Table 4.1, and it can be seen to agree very well with the simulation results of Peterson. An example of a run using non-random data (identifiers taken from the Algorithms published in the *Communications of the A.C.M.*) is also given in Table 4.1. It will be noticed that because of correlation effects between neighbouring entries, non-uniform mapping and non-random data, the figures of Peterson and of Schay and Spruth were not obtained. However, the results shown were fairly typical of a large number of runs where not too much attention was paid to producing the best mapping function. Peterson, using IBM Data Files, produced similar results.

It is important to notice that figures obtained for average length of search are independent of table size, and depend only on how full the table is. The surprising result is that with the table 80 per cent full the average length of search is still around 3.

So far all that has been examined is the value of $A(\sigma)$. The value of $T(\sigma)$, the genuine average length of search noting the frequency with which each entry is accessed, may be considerably less than $A(\sigma)$ if the entries required most frequently are entered first in the table.

		$A(\sigma)$	
σ	Peterson	Schay and Spruth	ACM Algorithms
·1	1·053	1·056	
·2	1·137	1·125	1·43
·3	1·230	1·214	
·4	1·366	1·333	2·35
·5	1·541	1·500	
·6	1·823	1·750	3·24
·7	2·260	2·167	
·8	3·223	3·000	5·22
·9	5·526	5·500	
1·0	16·914	∞	14·67

Table 4.1

An example of this can be seen in Batson (1965) where a symbol table for Algol identifiers together with the Algol reserved words is defined as an open hash table with the reserved words entered first.

One problem with a hash table of this kind is what to do when the table is full. Various suggestions have appeared which take special action for the additional entries such as having an additional table which is accessed after the hash. Another approach is to alter the mapping function so that the table can be enlarged and still leave the keys already entered in the same positions. Alterations of this kind usually produce a non-uniform mapping function which cause the average search length to go up. The simplest and, as it turns out, most efficient method is to increase the size of the table and re-hash all the entries into the new table. For example, if the original table was of length M and the new table is $2M$ in length, then suppose that it is decided to increase the size of the table when the original table becomes 80 per cent full. A measure of how much extra work will have been done in the re-hashing procedure will be to assume that after the re-hash each of the entries is accessed once more. A comparison of the time taken for accessing all the entries, assuming that the re-hashing had not taken place, with the time taken after the re-hash together with the time for the re-hash will give a measure of how much work is involved.

If it is 80 per cent full then the time for accessing each entry once, assuming no re-hashing, will be $N \times 3.223$ using Peterson's simulation figures. The time taken to re-hash is not very well expressed in terms of search-length. The entries in the old table can be removed serially so that the search length for picking up a key can be assumed to be 1. The search length for doing the re-hash will be 1.366 on average (using the 40 per cent full figure for the new table). Accessing each entry once more will be $1.366\ N$.

Therefore, continuing to use the old table would have cost $3.223\ N$ compared with $3.732\ N$ for re-hashing. These two times are so similar that obviously the cost of the re-hash is soon absorbed by the decrease in the search length for new entries and subsequent accesses to the original entries. These will now have an average search length of 1.366 instead of 3.223.

The question of when to re-hash has been glossed over in the above discussion. A fuller discussion can be found in Hopgood (1968).

4.5.2 Overflow hash

In the open hash method, overflow entries are inserted in the first empty neighbour. An alternative would be to have a completely separate table into which the overflow entries are inserted. If the number of overflow entries is small, then a look-up table could be used for this purpose. The method is only practical if the number of overflow entries is small.

4.5.3. Overflow with chaining

A variation of the *overflow* method described above is to have a separate overflow table for each position of the hash table. This subsidiary table can be thought of as a simple table look-up, although it would normally be organised as a single area of storage with pointers passing down the chain of entries associated with any position in the hash table. This is shown in the diagram Fig. 4.2. The zeros in the overflow table are used to represent the end of the chain from a particular entry. In this case the average scan length, assuming randomly distributed data, is

$$A(N,M) = 1 + \frac{(N-1)}{2M}$$

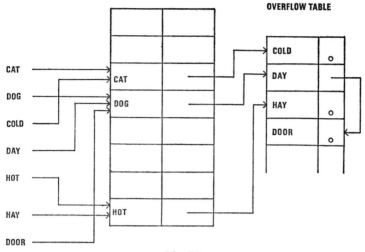

HASH TABLE

OVERFLOW TABLE

Fig. 4.2

4.5.4 *Overflow with internal chaining*

The two methods described above require a subsidiary overflow table. In general, if $N \leqslant M$ then there is in fact space in the original hash table to store the overflow entries. A variation of the *overflow with chaining* technique is called *overflow with internal chaining* where the overflow entries are chained into the empty positions of the hash table itself. Chaining in the overflow entries cannot of course be done until the hash table has been filled with all of its entries as, until this moment, the unused entries are not known. Production of the table is, therefore, in two parts. Initially only non-overflow entries are stored in the hash table (in our example CAT, DOG and HOT). Once it is known that no new entries will be added, the overflow entries, which have been temporarily stored in an overflow table, are chained into the empty positions. This could be done serially from the top as in Fig. 4.3. The average length of search is obviously identical to the *overflow with chaining*, that is:

$$A(N,M) = 1 + \frac{(N-1)}{2M}$$

The surprising result is that the table can be completely filled and the average length of search will still be less than 1·5. Also, if the non-overflow positions are filled with the most frequently required entries, then the average length of search $T(N,M)$ can be reduced even further. Its drawback is, of course, that, as the complete structure of the table cannot be determined until all entries are known, it is not

25

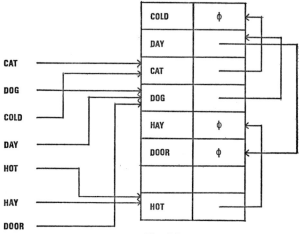

Fig. 4.3

very useful for tables where new entries are constantly being added (for example, identifier symbol tables). Its main use is, therefore, for pre-loaded tables which are only going to be accessed. This method is particularly useful in, for example, the *mnemonic-machine code conversion table* of an assembler or a table for looking-up reserved words. Some efforts have been made to use this kind of hash table for a conventional table where entries are constantly being added. Overflow entries are filled in at empty positions chosen at random and chained to their key position. If a later key required this position as its key position, then the overflow entry is moved to another empty position. The overhead for moving elements around means that it is difficult to give an estimate for the average search length in this method.

4.5.5 *Deletion of entries*

In some tables used, it may be necessary to delete entries from the table. In the hash methods, especially the open hash, it does modify the algorithm. In our example if it was decided that the entry COLD was no longer required, then the action required is not simply to change the entry COLD back to empty. If this was done, the entry DAY could no longer be accessed. Therefore, a subsidiary field of one bit is required which is the deleted entry marker. This would be set on when the entry is deleted. On accessing the key k, position $I(k)$ and its neighbours will be checked until either a match is found or an empty entry encountered. During the scan of $I(k)$ and its neighbours, the first entry with the deleted marker set is remembered. If this is a new entry then, instead of being added to the empty position, it will overwrite the first deleted entry position if there is one. With deletions the average length of search $A(N,M)$ will, of course, go up as at any time there will be deleted entries on some of the access paths.

4.5.6 *Mapping functions*

So far, little has been said about how to obtain a mapping function $I(k)$ for a key k. This depends to a large extent on the peculiarities of the keys concerned so that it is difficult to talk in generalities. It is important to remember that the calculation of $I(k)$ is an overhead on top of the length of search and that if the time required to calculate $I(k)$ is equivalent to a search time of length 5, then 5 must be added to all our figures for accessing hash tables. If a slightly worse mapping function could be obtained in a search time of length 1 then it is unlikely that this will increase the average length of scan by a value of 4. Consequently it is important to remember how much work is being done in calculating the mapping function compared with the amount of work done in scanning an entry. In general, a slightly worse mapping function which could be obtained much more quickly is usually desirable. The exception to this is where the hash table is on some secondary storage device and access time is very large. This is usually the case when hash tables are being used for file manipulation. In this case much care should be taken over the mapping function [see Buchholz, 1963)]. In compilers the table will normally reside in primary storage, and there is then a good case for producing the mapping function very quickly.

Consider the example of designing a mapping function for a hash table of size 128. The table is to be used as a symbol table for storage and accessing of identifiers defined in a Fortran subroutine. The identifiers must start with a letter and can be followed by one to five more letters or digits. This gives us more than 26×36^5 possible identifiers to be mapped into 128 entries called 0 to 127. The identifiers are available in the computer as a set of octal digits, two digits per character.

> A to Z are represented by 41 to 72 octal.
> 0 to 9 are represented by 20 to 31 octal.
> Space is represented by 01 octal.

The identifier CAT2 would be represented by:

$$434164220101$$

As the table is of 128 entries a mapping function is required which will produce as a result seven binary digits, and the aim is for the possible entries to be spread uniformly over the table positions.

The simplest method that could be adopted would be to truncate the binary number to the top seven bits giving in the above example 1000111 as the result of the mapping function. Looking at the definition of identifier, however, it will be noticed that the first character has to be a letter and all letters have the top most bit set to 1. Consequently, choosing this mapping function would mean that only entries 64 to 127 would be mapped on to by this function. This is obviously not uniform and a better choice would be to *extract* the seven bits after the initial bit, that is 0001110. This is obviously a lot better. In this case, an identifier with one of the first fifteen letters of the alphabet would be mapped on to the first half and the remaining eleven in to the second half. Another possibility would be to remove the top five digits and extract the next seven. In this case the split would be equal between the first and second halves of the table. However, as it is fairly frequent that single letter identifiers appear, it may be that quite an amount of useful information has been thrown away by this method. As can be seen this changing and adjusting of the mapping function can be carried out until a good balance is obtained, but it may well be that the cost gets exhorbitant in the meantime.

Another technique used to get information about the lower characters of an identifier to play a part is one called *folding*. Here the second half of the identifier would be added to the first giving 654265 as the new key and extracting from there.

A third possibility is *division*. For example, the octal number 434164220101 could be divided by the decimal number 127 and the remainder taken. This will give a fairly even distribution over the range 0 to 126 at the price of a division. If the time to do the division is small then this may well be the most desirable method to choose.

5

LANGUAGE DESCRIPTION

5.1 Introduction

Before describing the lexical and syntax analysis of the compiler, it is necessary to define some notation for describing the syntax of a programming language and some classification scheme for different types of languages. Most of the work described here derives from the work of Chomsky (1959) in the field of natural languages. The standard method adopted for describing a language is a *generative* scheme whereby a procedure is given for producing all the legal sentences of the language. An alternative approach would be to have a recogniser which could decide whether or not a sentence was legal. This alternative is seldom used in practice for defining a language but does closely resemble the syntax analysis phase of a compiler.

5.2 Notation

An example from the definition of English sentences will help to describe the notation adopted. An English *sentence* might be defined as a *subject phrase* followed by a *verb phrase*. The *subject phrase* might consist of the word 'the' followed by a *noun*. The *verb phrase* could be defined as a *verb* followed by an *object phrase*. The *object phrase* might consist of an *article* followed by a *noun*. The italics have been used here to denote syntactic elements that have been described in the above sentences. A subset of the complete set of English sentences could be defined by allowing only the nouns 'man' and 'dog', the verb 'has' and the articles 'a' and 'the'. The words in inverted commas are English words which will actually appear in the English sentence produced and are therefore given the name *terminal symbols*.

The notation adopted for describing these constructs is:

1	⟨sentence⟩	→	⟨subject phrase⟩ ⟨verb phrase⟩
2	⟨subject phrase⟩	→	the ⟨noun⟩
3	⟨verb phrase⟩	→	⟨verb⟩ ⟨object phrase⟩
4	⟨object phrase⟩	→	⟨article⟩ ⟨noun⟩
5	⟨verb⟩	→	has
6	⟨article⟩	→	a
7	⟨article⟩	→	the
8	⟨noun⟩	→	man
9	⟨noun⟩	→	dog

In this notation the syntactic elements are enclosed by '⟨' and '⟩'. An English *sentence* is *produced* by taking the element ⟨sentence⟩ and recursively replacing the left hand sides of rules by the equivalent right hand sides until a form is obtained containing no more syntactic elements but only words in the language. Rules of this form are often called *productions*. The sentence 'the man has a dog' would be obtained by starting from ⟨sentence⟩ and using the following productions:

Production used	
	⟨sentence⟩
1	⟨subject phrase⟩ ⟨verb phrase⟩
2	the ⟨noun⟩ ⟨verb phrase⟩
3	the ⟨noun⟩ ⟨verb⟩ ⟨object phrase⟩
4	the ⟨noun⟩ ⟨verb⟩ ⟨article⟩ ⟨noun⟩
9	the ⟨noun⟩ ⟨verb⟩ ⟨article⟩ dog
8	the man ⟨verb⟩ ⟨article⟩ dog
5	the man has ⟨article⟩ dog
6	the man has a dog

Note that there are many different orders in which the productions can be used to produce the sentence 'the man has a dog' from the syntactic element ⟨sentence⟩. The one chosen was not the most obvious just to emphasise this point.

For brevity, the syntactic elements enclosed between '⟨' and '⟩' will in future be written as single upper case letters while terminal symbols will always be written as lower case letters. Another name often given to the syntactic elements is the rather obvious one of *non-terminal symbols*.

The above example in the abbreviated notation would be:

$$1 \quad S \to P\,Q$$
$$2 \quad P \to \text{the } N$$
$$3 \quad Q \to V\,O$$
$$4 \quad O \to A\,N$$
$$5 \quad V \to \text{has}$$
$$6 \quad A \to a$$
$$7 \quad A \to \text{the}$$
$$8 \quad N \to \text{man}$$
$$9 \quad N \to \text{dog}$$

Starting from the non-terminal S several intermediate strings containing both non-terminal and terminal symbols are obtained before finally producing 'the man has a dog'. These intermediate forms together with the final string 'the man has a dog' are given the name *sentential forms*. In the example:

the N V A dog

is a sentential form. From now on, lower case Greek letters will be used to represent sentential forms.

The *grammar* of a language, then, consists of a set of productions having a unique non-terminal symbol, say S, which appear only on the left-hand side of productions. All the sentential forms containing no non-terminal symbols which can be produced from S will be the legal sentences obtainable in this language. The general form of productions allowed is:

$$\alpha \rightarrow \beta$$

where both α and β represent sentential forms. If during the enumeration of legal sentences a sentential form is obtained with the form α as a substring then another form can be produced by replacing α by β.

5.3 Chomsky classification

The type of language obtained when productions of the form:

$$\alpha \rightarrow \beta$$

appear in the definition of the grammar, with no restrictions existing on the sentential forms α and β, has been given the title Type 0 by Chomsky. This language type is much too general for computer languages although it is still unable to cope with natural English.

Chomsky defined several other classes of language each of which is a subset of the previous class.

The Chomsky Type 1 language is one where the productions are restricted to:

$$\alpha A\beta \rightarrow \alpha\pi\beta$$

where A is a single non-terminal symbol, π is not null and α,β,π are sentential forms. Languages in this class are often given the name *context sensitive*.

A Chomsky Type 2 language is one where the productions are restricted to the form

$$A \rightarrow \pi$$

that is, the left hand side consists of only one non-terminal symbol. Most programming languages approximate to the classification Chomsky Type 2. The notation BNF [Naur *et al.* (1960)] is equivalent to the definition given above for Chomsky Type 2, so that the language Algol which is defined by the notation BNF is of Chomsky Type 2.

With languages in use today which do not correspond to Chomsky Type 2, it is usually possible at the lexical scan to alter these languages into this form if they have only minor inconsistences. Most of the discussion of translator techniques will assume that the language is either Type 2 or a subset of this class.

The Chomsky Type 3 languages are ones where productions are restricted to the form:

$$A \to a$$
$$A \to aB$$

that is, the right hand sides must consist of only a terminal symbol or a terminal symbol followed by a non-terminal symbol. The Type 3 languages coincide with the finite state languages and most of the work done at the lexical scan will be on parts of the program defined as a finite state language.

5.4 Parsing

As shown already, it is possible to decide whether one sentential form can be produced from another by taking the initial sentential form and enumerating all sentential forms obtainable from this form by repeated use of the productions defined in the grammar. Given a sentential form α and a second form β, then α *directly produces* β if and only if

$$\alpha = \gamma A \delta$$

and

$$\beta = \gamma \pi \delta$$

and there is a production $A \to \pi$. Conversely β *directly reduces* into α.

Similarly, α *produces* β and β *reduces* into α if and only if there exists a sequence of sentential forms such that:

'α directly produces α_1, α_1 directly produces α_2, ...,
α_{n-1} directly produces α_n, α_n directly produces β.'

Given that a sentential form α produces a form β, then a *parse* of the string β with respect to α is a sequence of numbers defining the productions that apply at each stage in reducing β into α.

In the example, the sentence 'the man has a dog' has a parse with respect to ⟨sentence⟩ of [6.5.8.9.4.3.2.1]. Note that this parse is not well defined in all cases. For example the sentence 'the man has a man' might have a parse [6.5.8.8.4.3.2.1] in which case it would not be obvious which of the words 'man' was being reduced to ⟨noun⟩ in the two uses of production 8.

Therefore a *canonical parse* is defined which starts at the left hand end of the sentential form β and first applies the production which reduces the characters furthest to the left first. This then produces a second sentential form, and the process is repeated until α is obtained. The canonical parse in our example would be:

$$[8.2.5.6.9.4.3.1]$$

The sub-string which is reduced by the first reduction in the canonical parse is called the *handle* of the sentential form. In the example, the handle of the sentence is 'man'.

A language is said to be *unambiguous* if there exists only one canonical parse for every sentence in the language. Given a grammar, it can be shown that, in general, there is no algorithm for deciding whether or not the grammar is ambiguous. If, in the example, a production also existed of the form:

$$\langle\text{subject phrase}\rangle \rightarrow \text{the man}$$

then the sentence in the example could be parsed in two different ways, namely:

$$\langle\text{subject phrase}\rangle \rightarrow \text{the } \langle\text{noun}\rangle$$
$$\langle\text{noun}\rangle \qquad\qquad \rightarrow \text{man}$$

or,

$$\langle\text{subject phrase}\rangle \rightarrow \text{the man}$$

So far, assuming it is known how the initial sentential form produces the final form, then the canonical parse can be defined. This does not mean, however, that, given the final sentential form and the set of productions defining the grammar, the canonical parse can be produced. This is the problem to be solved by the syntax analysis phase of the compiler.

Some of the problems can be seen in the following example:

Suppose the sentence 'the man has a dog' is to be parsed. The initial 'the' could have been produced by production 7. Production 8 would recognize 'man' as a noun, giving us the reduced form '$\langle\text{article}\rangle \langle\text{noun}\rangle$ has a dog'. This would be reduced by 4 to '$\langle\text{object phrase}\rangle$ has a dog'. It would not be until this point that no production could be applied, and it would then be necessary to go back and try an alternative approach. The organisation of such *back-tracking* will be one of the main concerns of some of the parsers to be described in the chapter on syntax analysis.

Expressing it another way, the problem of parsing is to find the handle of the sentential form at each stage of the reduction process.

5.5 Recursion

Before closing this chapter it is necessary to define some more terms concerned with recursion. A language is said to be *directly left recursive* if productions of the form:

$$A \rightarrow A\alpha$$

exist in the grammar.

A language is said to be *directly right recursive* if productions of the form:

$$A \rightarrow \alpha A$$

exist in the grammar.

A language is said to be *directly self embedding* if rules of the form:

$$A \rightarrow \alpha A \beta$$

exist in the grammar. Similar definitions exist for left recursion, right recursion, and self embedding.

6

LEXICAL ANALYSIS

6.1 Introduction

The aim of the lexical analysis phase of the compiler is to take the input program, which is presented to the compiler in some arbitrary form, and translate this into a string of characters which will be called the *S-string*. This is the input to the syntax analyser. The S-string should consist of grammatically correct sentences belonging to a language (the S-language) which can be analysed by the parser provided in the syntax analysis phase. The S-language will normally be of Chomsky Type 2 or a subset of this class, depending on the type of parser to be used.

The lexical analyser could of course produce many different S-languages which satisfy this criterion. It is therefore important to remember two other desirable properties of the S-language. First, the grammatical classes existing in the syntax of the S-language should be closely linked to the semantic meaning of the strings defined in the class. For example, $A + B*C$ in Fortran should be parsed as $A + \langle B * C \rangle$ but not as $\langle A + B \rangle * C$. Sometimes the lexical analyser can aid the syntax analyser to do this by conversion or rearranging of characters. Secondly, the grammar of the S-language should be uniform in the sense that the majority of syntactic structures contained in the S-language should also require the same type of parsing algorithm as the whole language. For example, it would be unreasonable for the lexical analyser to have as output an S-language which was of Chomsky Type 2 apart from one construct which made it of Chomsky Type 1, especially if the S-language could easily be altered by the lexical analyser to resolve the anomaly.

For example, Algol can be defined as a precedence grammar [see Floyd (1963)] apart from the two uses of ':' as a label delimiter and also in the array declaration. If the lexical analyser is able to change the internal form of one of the uses, so that the two uses are distinct symbols to the syntax analyser, then a precedence grammar parser may be used rather than a more general and less efficient parser. This is a fairly trivial problem at the lexical level as the array use always occurs between the symbol **'array'** and the following semicolon.

At the other extreme, it may be that parts of the language fall into the class Chomsky Type 3 which can easily be analysed at the lexical level. For example, it is usual for the lexical analyser to pack-up identifiers into a single symbol and floating point constants into the numerical value. If left to the syntax analyser, this will probably be done inefficiently. Similarly basic symbols in the programming language, which, because of hardware deficiencies, are represented by several characters on the external media, should be converted to single characters in the S-language. For example, the Algol reserved words such as **begin** should be recognised at the lexical level and converted to a single symbol.

6.2 Line reconstruction and input conversion

The input to a compiler will vary considerably from computer to computer and may well be different for two compilers on the same computer. Consequently this section must be a generalisation of the situation in any particular environment. Frequently the input to the compiler is a program punched on paper tape or cards and presented to the computer via some peripheral device. In this case, the characters presented to the lexical analyser as input closely resemble the binary numbers obtained by considering a punched hole as equivalent to a binary '1'. Alternatively there may be some supervisory system that converts the input to a form independent of the peripheral equipment before passing it to the compiler. The input may be provided a character at a time, a line at a time or even the whole program.

If characters are being provided to the lexical analyser from the peripheral equipment one at a time, then it is likely that the numerical values of holes punched on tape or cards do not have much resemblance to the numerical values desired for characters in the S-language. However, many characters on the input have a 1−1 correspondence with characters appearing in the S-language. Consequently it is usually desirable to have a *conversion table* producing internal forms of the characters as they are read from the input. These characters will belong to a language called the L-language, and the aim of the conversion will be to make characters in the L-language and S-language the same where this 1 − 1 correspondence exists. For example, the external forms of the operators '+' and '−' on the input media might be the punched codes 01011 and 11010 on five-hole paper tape. The S-language might require these to be the numerical values 28 and 29 in which case the conversion table would ensure that these values were the ones for '+' and '−' in the L-language.

As the number of unused punch configurations on a paper tape, for example, is not high, it is normal to use a direct access table for achieving the character conversion. The conversion table may be divided into several parts corresponding to different states of the input stream, and the look-up in the conversion table is done in the

36

part of the table corresponding to the state. For example a five-hole paper tape only has 32 different hole configurations. In order to increase the number of possible characters available, two of the hole configurations are defined as the control characters *figure shift* and *letter shift*. Hole configurations then represent one of two characters depending on which was the last control character to be punched on the tape previous to this character.

The conversion table could be set up with each entry having two parts. The first part contains the *L-form* of the character, and the second contains a pointer to a *small routine* which is entered after the conversion and defines any special action to be taken. In the example, the most common small routine would be one which would go back to analyse the next character after dealing with the one converted. The table would consist of 64 entries with the *case pointer* set either at the start (for figure shift say) or half way down. The entry in the conversion table looked at would be the '*m*'th one after the case pointer, if the numerical value of the character was '*m*'. When the characters' *figure shift or letter shift* were read, the relevant position in the conversion table would point to a small routine which would reset the position of the case pointer. Redundant characters on the input such as *runout* and *erases* could be removed by small routines which immediately returned for the next character.

It has been assumed, so far, that characters, once converted, could be passed on one at a time to be analysed. However, certain peripheral devices exist which allow the carriage to be moved by a *backspace* key. This allows overprinting of characters and also allows the position of characters in the input line to be different from the order in which they appear on the input tape. For example the word 'as' could appear on the input as:

space s *backspace backspace* a

In this case a line image equivalent to the original print out on the peripheral device must be formed before analysis can take place. This is called *line-reconstruction*. A buffer allowing several entries in each character position of the line needs to be set up with a pointer P to the current position reached across the line and a second pointer M giving the maximum length of line reached so far. The normal small routine pointed at by the conversion table will then store the character in the buffer at position P and advance the position of P. The pointer M could be updated every time P is increased, or alternatively it is more efficient to reset it only when P is decreased. This can be done by the small routine associated with the backspace character. In this case the final value of M is $max(P,M)$. The number of characters allowed in any position will be two or three (overprinting more than three characters is unlikely as the print out would become unreadable). As it is not possible to decide in which order

37

two overprinted characters have arrived, the entries in any buffer position must be re-ordered into some standard form such as numerically ascending order. This will guarantee that $\neq$ punched as '= *backspace* /' and '/ *backspace* =' are recognised as the same character. The problems attached to line reconstruction are all concerned with making the internal buffer equivalent to what the user sees on the print-out of his program. If the user overprints a character by itself, should this be a different symbol? If a backspace is attempted at the start of a line, what happens on the punching device? Should a character printed over an erase be ignored? What are the tab settings on the device so that these can be followed internally? Once the line image has been obtained, the lexical analysis is the same as for the normal input straight from the conversion table.

6.3 Lexical conversion

So far, the conversion table has produced an L-string which, in the case of characters having a $1 - 1$ correspondence between the input character and S-character, has the L-character equal to the S-character. Otherwise the conversion table has produced an L-character which will be in the most reasonable form for the lexical analyser.

For example, the composite Algol symbols such as **begin** are delimited in most input forms by marking the letters of the symbol in some way. Frequently the individual letters are underlined. The lexical analyser in this case can recognise the start of an Algol composite symbol by the underlining of the initial letter. Therefore, this concept can be extended so that the conversion table marks (underlines) all characters that could start a composite Algol symbol. A dialect having a non-escape underline, which would present **begin** as _b_e_g_i_n, could have the conversion table ignoring the underlined characters apart from remembering that the next character had to be marked as underlined. Similarly **begin** written as 'begin' could have the primes changing the pointer to a conversion table so that the look-up of input characters would be in a part of the input table which converted characters to the marked form. The final prime would reset the pointer in the conversion table. In most Algol dialects, however, there will be a non-empty set of composite symbols which are not already marked in this way. For example, the Algol symbol ':=' often appears as ':' followed by '=', and the exponentiation sign often appears as '**'. The conversion table should therefore set underline markers on : and *.

The recognition process can then be described as follows:

(a) If next character is not underlined then convert as simple symbol.

(b) If next character is underlined then check L-string against

38

entries in the *composite symbol table* to see if a match is found. If a match is found pass on relevant S-character.

(c) If no match is found convert first character as simple symbol.

Rule (c) ensures that, for example, ':' not followed by '=' is recognised as ':'. At step (b) the table look-up would probably be in a hash table with the composite symbols preloaded into it. An open hash or overflow with internal chaining would be the most usual method to use. As the conversion table gives complete control over the form of the entries, an average search length very close to 1 should be obtained. A full description of the lexical analyser for an Algol compiler is given by Hopgood and Bell (1967). It is important to notice that in extending the lexical analyser to accept an additional hardware representation of the input, all that is required is an additional conversion table with possibly minor extensions to the composite symbol table.

Apart from the recognition of the Algol symbols, it is probably desirable to also pack up identifiers appearing in the program so that all that is passed is an S-character representing the position in the table where the identifier is stored. It is important to realise that this process is in no way connected with storage allocation for the identifier. It should be thought of as a process for replacing many character identifiers by single character identifiers. In Algol this same identifier name may be used for several different variables in different blocks. It is the task of the syntax analyser and associated semantic routines to discover this structure of the program and allocate storage.

The identifiers could be looked up and entered in a separate hash table usually called the *symbol table*. However, it is also possible for the composite symbol table for the Algol symbols to also be *the* symbol table. The basic Algol symbols are preloaded into the table and identifiers added as they appear. This ensures rapid access to the basic Algol symbols [see Batson (1965)]. Some dialects have no special delimiters for the Algol basic symbols, and they are only recognised by assuming they have reserved names which cannot be used as identifiers. In this case the recognition of Algol basic symbols and identifiers is almost identical

6.4 Number conversion

A good example of a Chomsky Type 3 subset of a language is usually the structure of floating point constants in the language. The Algol definition of a floating point number is given in the report as follows:

⟨unsigned number⟩	→	⟨decimal number⟩
⟨unsigned number⟩	→	⟨exponent part⟩
⟨unsigned number⟩	→	⟨decimal number⟩ ⟨exponent part⟩
⟨decimal number⟩	→	⟨unsigned integer⟩
⟨decimal number⟩	→	⟨decimal fraction⟩
⟨decimal number⟩	→	⟨unsigned integer⟩ ⟨decimal fraction⟩
⟨unsigned integer⟩	→	⟨digit⟩
⟨unsigned integer⟩	→	⟨unsigned integer⟩ ⟨digit⟩
⟨decimal fraction⟩	→	· ⟨unsigned integer⟩
⟨exponent part⟩	→	10 ⟨integer⟩
⟨integer⟩	→	⟨unsigned integer⟩
⟨integer⟩	→	+ ⟨unsigned integer⟩
⟨integer⟩	→	− ⟨unsigned integer⟩

As it stands this is not Chomsky Type 3. However, it is a simple matter to change the rules to the following set:

⟨unsigned number⟩	→ *digit* ⟨rest unsigned number⟩
⟨unsigned number⟩	→ · ⟨decimal fraction⟩
⟨unsigned number⟩	→ 10 ⟨exponent part⟩
⟨rest unsigned number⟩	→ *digit* ⟨rest unsigned number⟩
⟨rest unsigned number⟩	→ · ⟨decimal fraction⟩
⟨rest unsigned number⟩	→ 10 ⟨exponent part⟩
⟨rest unsigned number⟩	→ Λ
⟨decimal fraction⟩	→ *digit* ⟨rest decimal fraction⟩
⟨rest decimal fraction⟩	→ Λ
⟨rest decimal fraction⟩	→ 10 ⟨exponent part⟩
⟨rest decimal fraction⟩	→ *digit* ⟨rest decimal fraction⟩
⟨exponent part⟩	→ *sign* ⟨exponent integer⟩
⟨exponent part⟩	→ *digit* ⟨rest exponent integer⟩
⟨exponent integer⟩	→ *digit* ⟨rest exponent integer⟩
⟨rest exponent integer⟩	→ *digit* ⟨rest exponent integer⟩
⟨rest exponent integer⟩	→ Λ

The character Λ is used here to denote a null character. It is easily seen that these productions conform to the definition of Chomsky Type 3. As stated previously, a language expressed in this form can be parsed by a finite state algorithm. The number of states required coincides with the number of syntactic classes to define the language. Table 6.1 gives a *state table* for a recogniser for the numbers. The process is started in state 1, and the character appearing on the input stream defines the state into which the recogniser is to move. The null symbol can be assumed to include all other characters that could appear after the number. A number is recognised if one of the *exit* positions is reached. Non-recognition occurs if a blank entry is encountered. For example recognition of 1·45 Λ would proceed as follows:

INPUT STATE	CHARACTER	NEW STATE
1	1	2
2	.	3
3	4	4
4	5	4
4	Λ	EXIT

If each entry in the state table also contains a pointer to a small routine to be executed, then the calculation of the numerical value of the constant proceeds in parallel with the recognition. Table 6.2 gives the form of the augmented state table where the small routines are as follows:

$$V: \quad A = 10\,A + d$$
$$W: \quad n = n + 1$$
$$A = 10\,A + d$$
$$X: \quad E = 10\,E + d$$
$$Y: \quad A = 1$$
$$Z: \quad e = sign$$

	digit	.	10	±	
1 ⟨unsigned number⟩	2	3	5		
2 ⟨rest unsigned number⟩	2	3	5		EXIT
3 ⟨decimal fraction⟩	4				
4 ⟨rest decimal fraction⟩	4		5		EXIT
5 ⟨exponent part⟩	7			6	
6 ⟨exponent integer⟩	7				
7 ⟨rest exponent integer⟩	7				EXIT

Table 6.1

On entry $A = n = E = 0$; e = '+'

	digit = d	.	10	±	
1 ⟨unsigned number⟩	2, V	3	5, Y		
2 ⟨rest unsigned number⟩	2, V	3	5		EXIT
3 ⟨decimal fraction⟩	4, W				
4 ⟨rest decimal fraction⟩	4, W		5		EXIT
5 ⟨exponent part⟩	7, X			6, Z	
6 ⟨exponent integer⟩	7, X				
7 ⟨rest exponent integer⟩	7, X				EXIT

Exit, Number $= A \times 10^{eE-n}$

Table 6.2

In these routines 'd' stands for the digit encountered. The parameters are initialised to:

$A = 0$ value of mantissa ignoring decimal point
$n = 0$ number of decimal places
$E = 0$ exponent
$e = +$ exponent sign

The procedure will exit with the value of the constant being $A \times 10^{eE-n}$.

Rewriting Chomsky Type 3 subsets of the language as finite state tables is straightforward but may be wasteful in space if the number of empty (error) positions is high. This can be useful if different diagnostics are required at every error position. Each empty position coincides with an explicit error in the format of the number, and it does enable good diagnostics to be obtained. For example the second entry in state 3 could give the diagnostic:

TWO CONSECUTIVE DECIMAL POINTS
APPEAR IN NUMBER

As precise diagnostics can be given, it is also often possible to define the correct recovery action.

A different notation for defining finite state recognisers has been called the *syntax machine* by Glennie (1960). The equivalent recogniser written as a syntax machine is given in Fig. 6.1. Unless otherwise denoted by arrows, flow of control is 'left to right' or downwards. Comparators are enclosed in circles. The **true** exit is horizontal and moves the input on one character. The **false** exit is downwards and does not alter the input.

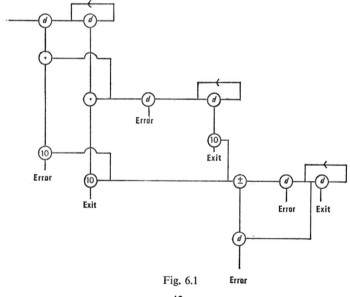

Fig. 6.1   Error

42

The virtue of the syntax machine is that it is useful for defining recognisers for strings that do not fit easily into any class. In particular, recognisers can be defined which are more efficient as far as storage is concerned. Fig. 6.2 gives a modified syntax machine for recognising numbers. False exits not marked are error exits. This machine can then be translated into a set of instructions for doing the testing, or alternatively written in tabular form (see Table 6.3). The machine starts in state 1 and exits **true** or **false** to the state defined, depending on whether recognition takes place with the character defined for that state. Before the next state is examined the relevant action is taken. The small routines and initialisation coincide exactly with those for the finite state table.

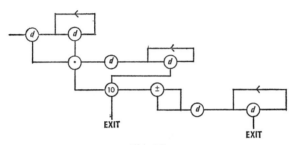

Fig. 6.2

State	Character	Next State if True	Action if True	Next State if False	Action if False
1	d	2	V	3	
2	d	2	V	3	
3	.	4		6	
4	d	5	W	Error	
5	d	5	W	6	
6	10	7		Exit	
7	±	8	Z	8	
8	d	9	X	Error	
9	d	9	X	Exit	

Table 6.3

6.5 A lexical analyser for Fortran

The discussion of Algol has shown the role of the lexical analyser in a language with a precise syntactic structure. The main concern has been the conversion of Algol composite symbols into single characters in the S-language. Fortran is normally punched on cards and the character set is usually restricted to the 48 characters in the original card code set. Consequently some characters are over-worked with the same character being used in many different syntactic

43

positions. If possible the lexical analyser should convert the different uses of the same character into distinct characters in the S-language.

Once it has been discovered that a basic Fortran statement is not an assignment statement, it is possible to recognise any Fortran statement by its initial characters. The reason for the proviso on the assignment statement first being recognised is because the following are all legal assignment statements:

$$DO\ 10\ I = 1$$
$$IF\ (I) = 3$$
$$CALL\ AB\ (I,J) = 4$$

A simple way to recognise an assignment statement is that it has no zero-level commas on the right hand side of a zero-level '=' sign. This information can be obtained by the conversion table changing the pointer on encountering a zero level '=' to a part of the table which counts zero-level commas. This process also defines the DO statement as this is the only statement with '=' *and* zero-level commas. The remaining statements can now be recognised by comparing the particular statement with a list of the first few characters of the possible Fortran statements. As two of the most frequently found statements have already been recognised, a fairly simple look-up device is probably adequate. The S-form of the statement will probably consist of a character differentiating between the different types of statements followed by the characters of the statement.

It would be desirable to convert the ambiguous symbols to unique characters in the S-language but this is not always easy. For example the output statement:

$$PRINT\ 10,A,\ (B(I,\ J),\ C,\ J = 1,3),\ D,\ (E,F)$$

has the ',' used as a separator for list elements, lists, array subscripts, and DO parameters to mention just a few. This means that either the parser has to be carefully designed to differentiate between these different uses or the lexical analyser can do the conversion. The main objection to recognition by the lexical analyser is that arithmetic expressions can replace identifiers in several positions. This means that a bracket count must be kept to locate the end of an arithmetic expression. In a language like Fortran this may well be desirable as otherwise a more complex parser may be required at the syntax analysis phase. For example, Glennie's syntax machine with a subroutine for recognising arithmetic expressions could be used for this purpose.

7

SYNTAX ANALYSIS

7.1 Introduction

The main aim of the syntax analysis phase of the compiler is to take the S-string produced by the lexical analyser, and to use some parsing algorithm to verify that the S-string consists of a legal string or strings in the S-language. In addition, it will be required to collect information about the language, and produce as output a *C-structure* which could be code, which is ready to be executed or interpreted, but is more likely to be a structural representation of the S-string which will be used to generate code. The C-structure could, for example, be passed to an optimising phase which will modify the C-structure so that better code can be produced. For example, Fig. 7.1 shows two possible C-structures for the arithmetic expression $a + b*c$.

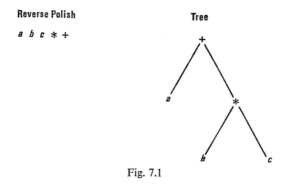

Reverse Polish

$a\ b\ c\ *\ +$

Tree

Fig. 7.1

The design and theory of parsing algorithms has grown enormously in recent years. Many are of only academic interest because of the impossibility of defining efficient computer programs for the algorithm. Only a few methods have been widely used in handwritten compilers. Other more general methods have only become evident in the compiler generator systems being produced where some efficiency has to be sacrificed so that the system can handle a variety of languages. The algorithms to be described here have all been used in hand-written compilers and in compiler generator systems.

7.2 Precedence grammars

Before describing the algorithm for parsing sentences in a language which is a *precedence grammar*, some additional syntactic definitions must be given. In section 5.4 the term *handle* of a sentential form was defined as the substring which is first reduced in the canonical parse. In the example subset of the English language defined in section 5.2, the sentence 'the man has a dog' had, at each step in the parse, the handles shown in Table 7.1. The symbols $<$ and $>$ have been used to

	sentential form				handle
the	$<$man$>$	has	a	dog	man
$<$the	N$>$	has	a	dog	the N
	P	$<$has$>$	a	dog	has
	P	V	$<$a$>$	dog	a
	P	V	A	$<$dog$>$	dog
	P	V	$<$A	N$>$	A N
	P	$<$V	O	$>$	V O
	$<$P		Q$>$		P Q
		S			

Table 7.1

delimit the handle from the rest of the sentence. Similarly the individual symbols in the handle can be delimited by the symbol $\doteq$. The original sentence could then be written:

$$\text{the} < \text{m} \doteq \text{a} \doteq \text{n} > \text{has a dog}$$

The relationships $<$, $\doteq$, $>$ can be thought of as existing between the two symbols that the operator delimits. In the example e $<$ m, m $\doteq$ a, and n $>$ h, for example. In order to simplify the meaning of the operators at the end of the sentential form, it is assumed to be enclosed in the symbols '$\vdash$' and '$\dashv$' which can be thought of as giving context to the sentential form. Therefore, for example, the relationship $\vdash$ $<$ P exists. Considering all the possible sentences, then the relationships given in Table 7.2 can be seen to exist between pairs of symbols. Apart from the two entries marked by '*', there is a unique relationship between pairs of symbols. The relationship between the pairs (e,m) and (e,d) can be both $<$ and $>$. This can be seen from the sentential form:

$$\vdash \text{the} < \text{d} \doteq \text{o} \doteq \text{g} > \text{has the dog} \dashv$$

which later in the reduction sequence has the handle given by:

$$\vdash \text{P V} < \text{t} \doteq \text{h} \doteq \text{e} > \text{dog} \dashv$$

A unique relationship between pairs of symbols can be obtained by replacing rule 2 by:

$$P \rightarrow no\ N$$

The relationship e ⋗ d and e ⋗ m then exist. A unique relationship therefore exists between pairs of symbols that can appear adjacent to each other in legal sentential forms.

	a	d	e	g	h	m	n	o	s	t	A	N	O	P	Q	S	V	⊣
⊢						⋖			⋖					⋖	⋖			
a		⋗				⋗	≐		≐									
d								≐										
e		*			*							≐						
g				⋗														⋗
h	≐		≐															
m	≐																	
n				⋗				≐										⋗
o		⋖	≐	⋖								≐						
s	⋗																	
t					≐													
A		⋖			⋖							≐						
N				⋗														⋗
O																		⋗
P				⋖											≐		⋖	
Q																		⋗
S																		⋗
V	⋖								⋖	⋖			≐					

Table 7.2

Finding the handle and therefore defining a parsing algorithm is now quite simple, assuming uniqueness of the relation between any two symbols. The sentential form is examined from left to right until a pair of symbols is found between which the relationship ⋗ holds. This position is noted and the sentential form is then examined from this point *leftwards* until the first two symbols with the relationship ⋖ are encountered. The set of symbols between ⋖ and ⋗ is the handle to be reduced. In the example:

⊢ no man has a dog ⊣

the relationships from left to right are:

$$\vdash \lessdot n \doteq o \lessdot m \doteq a \doteq n \gtrdot h \dots$$

Therefore the handle must be given by:

$$\lessdot m \doteq a \doteq n \gtrdot$$

which produces:

$$\vdash \lessdot n \doteq o \doteq N \gtrdot h \dots$$

Therefore the next handle is ' no N '. Notice that after the first reduction there can be no symbols with the relation ' $\gtrdot$ ' to the left of the point reached, so that the scan of the string from left to right to find the next occurrence of $\gtrdot$ may be started at the point reached so far. The definition of which *precedence relation* exists between a pair of symbols can be formalised as follows:

(1) The relationship $A \doteq B$ exists between two symbols, either of which can be terminal or non-terminal, if a production exists in the language of the form:

$$C \rightarrow \alpha A B \beta$$

where α,β are two sentential forms of which either or both may be null.

(2) The relationship $A \lessdot B$ exists between two symbols if a product exists in the language of the form:

$$C \rightarrow \alpha A \gamma \beta$$

and γ *produces* $B\pi$ for some string π.

(3) The relationship $A \gtrdot B$ exists between two symbols *either* if a production exists in the language of the form:

$$C \rightarrow \alpha \gamma B \beta$$

and γ *produces* πA for some string π

or if a production exists in the language of the form:

$$C \rightarrow \alpha \gamma \delta \beta$$

and γ *produces* μA, δ *produces* $B\pi$ for some strings μ and π.

The strings denoted by Greek letters may be null. A language where a unique relationship exists between all pairs of terminal and non-terminal symbols is called a *precedence grammar*.

This immediately leads us to a very simple and straightforward parsing algorithm for precedence grammars. The symbol $\vdash$ is inserted in the initial position of a stack, and characters from the input S-string are added to the stack one at a time as required. Each time a symbol is added to the stack, the relationship between the top two symbols is looked up. If the relationship is $\lessdot$ or $\doteq$, then the next symbol from the input S-string is added to the stack and the procedure repeated. If the relationship $\gtrdot$ exists between the top two symbols, then all symbols are removed between the top symbol and the first symbol of the pair of symbols that last had the relationship < between them. The symbols removed are replaced by the equivalent non-terminal symbol, and the process continues by examining the relationship between the top two symbols in the stack. For example the sentence 'no man has a dog' would be parsed as shown in Fig. 7.2.

```
                         ⊣
  h                      g
  n          a           o  ⊣
  a   h      s      d  d  N  ⊣
  m   N      a  a   a  A  A  O  ⊣
  o   o  h   h  V   V  V  V  V  O  ⊣
  n   n  P   P  P   P  P  P  P  P  S
  ⊢   ⊢  ⊢   ⊢  ⊢   ⊢  ⊢  ⊢  ⊢  ⊢  ⊢
```

Fig. 7.2

Symbols are added to the stack until the pair (n,h) appears in the stack. This is the first pair where n ≻ h. This causes symbol 'N' to be recognised. As N ≻ h, the reduction to the non-terminal P occurs immediately. The parsing then proceeds as shown.

A good example of a language with a precedence grammar, which is parsed in this way, is given in the papers on the language Euler by Wirth and Weber (1966).

7.3 Operator precedence grammars

An *operator grammar* is one where no productions of the form:

$$C \rightarrow \alpha A B \beta$$

occur, where A and B are both non-terminal symbols, and α, β are strings of symbols either or both of which may be null. For operator grammars, the relationships $\doteq$, < and > need only be defined between terminal symbols of the language as follows:
(1) a $\doteq$ b if there is a production

$$C \rightarrow \alpha a b \beta$$
or $$C \rightarrow \alpha a A b \beta$$

where A is non-terminal and the symbols a,b are terminal.
(2) a < b if there is a production
$$C \rightarrow \alpha a A \beta$$
and A *produces* bπ for some π or A *produces* Dbπ where D is non-terminal.
(3) a > b if there is a production
$$C \rightarrow \alpha A b \beta$$

and A *produces* πa for some π or A *produces* πaD where D is non-terminal.

An *operator precedence grammar* is an operator grammar where a unique relationship occurs between pairs of terminal symbols. These relationships are called the *precedence relations* of the terminal symbols.

7.4 A parser for an operator precedence grammar

Most computer languages can be altered by the lexical conversion so that the S-language has an operator precedence grammar and, as a parser for an operator precedence grammar is efficient and simple, it has therefore been widely used in compilers. Arithmetic expressions, which constitute the chief part of most scientific languages, will be used as examples in the analysis procedures to be discussed here. A simplified structure of arithmetic expressions in the S-language can be defined as:

1 $P \rightarrow (E)$
2 $P \rightarrow \langle \text{identifier} \rangle$
3 $E \rightarrow T$
4 $E \rightarrow E + T$
5 $T \rightarrow P$
6 $T \rightarrow T * P$

Subtraction and division behave in a similar manner to addition and multiplication, as far as the analysis is concerned, and so have been ignored in order to simplify the examples. Also the relationship between addition and multiplication resembles the relationship between multiplication and exponentiation. Consequently exponentiation has also been ignored and examples containing only addition and multiplication will be used.

Identifiers denoting variables will have had their individual letters and digits inserted in the symbol table, and the lexical scan of the expression will produce on the S-string in place of the identifier a pointer to the symbol table entry corresponding to the particular identifier name. Therefore, when an example S-string is written as $a + b*c$, the symbols a,b,c stand for pointers to the symbol table and these will be marked in some way to distinguish them from the symbols + and * which will be numeric values defining these operators.

These symbol table pointers tend to be very similar to non-terminal symbols, and it is not normally necessary to define precedence relations between the pointers and the terminal symbols such as + and *. They can be thought of as non-terminal symbols that have been produced in an 'ad hoc' fashion independent of the parser. It is as though the S-string to be parsed already contained non-

50

terminal symbols. Identifiers and non-terminal symbols will, in the context of arithmetic statements, be called *operands* and the terminal symbols will be called *operators*.

From the definitions of the simplified arithmetic expression, the precedence relations between the terminal symbols (operators) can be defined and stored in a table (see Fig. 7.3) called the *precedence table*. As the precedence relations only exist between the operators, it is more convenient to use a stack with two columns rather than the one column stack used in the case of precedence grammars. One column will have operators inserted in it, while the other will contain operands. This is mainly a notational device and could in practice be implemented as a one column stack. As the parsing depends on the top two operators at each stage, it is convenient to have these next to each other in the diagrams.

	+	*	(	)	⊣
⊢	⋖	⋖	⋖		
+	⋗	⋖	⋖	⋗	⋗
*	⋗	⋗	⋖	⋗	⋗
(	⋖	⋖	⋖	≐	
)	⋗	⋗		⋗	⋗

Fig. 7.3

From the definitions of an operator grammar it can be seen that the handle is delimited, as before, by the symbols ⋖ and ⋗, and the same algorithm applies for finding the handle as was used in the case of precence grammars. As the precedence relations only exist between terminal symbols, there is some doubt about whether the non-terminal symbols also occur in the handle. For example, if a ⋗ b then in the case a A b, should A be part of the handle? Looking at the definitions for ⋖ and ⋗ it is easily seen that

(1) if a ⋗ b, then a A b has the relationship:

$$a \, A \gtrdot b$$

(2) if a ⋖ b, then a A b has the relationship:

$$a \lessdot A \, b$$

Therefore on combination all operands between ⋖ and ⋗ will be part of the handle.

For example, the expression $\vdash a + b * (c + d) + e \dashv$ would be parsed by first loading $\vdash$ into the initial operator position of the stack and filling the stack until the next operator is encountered (see Fig. 7.4). Looking up the precedence relation ($\vdash, +$) in the precedence table will show that, as $\vdash \lessdot +$, the stack should be filled. The next operand and operator will be loaded (2) and, as $+ \lessdot *$, filling occurs again. The next character on the input is the operator (so that this will be loaded into the operator position (3) and, as $* \lessdot ($, filling will

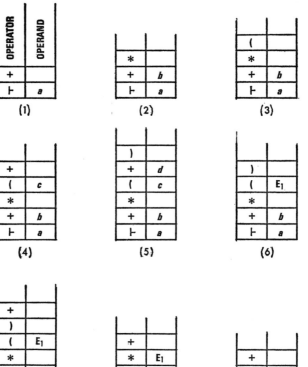

Fig. 7.4

52

occur once more until the top two operators are +) and where
+ >). Combination will now occur and, as (< +, the handle
must be $c + d$. This C-structure will be output (see Fig. 7.5) and the
stack will be collapsed (6) with the pointer E_1 to this C-structure
inserted in the stack. The top two operators now have the relation
($\doteq$) so that filling will occur (7). As) > + combination will occur
once more. In this case the handle is (E_1). This bracketing may be
inherent in the C-structure used and, in this case, no additional
structure is produced but instead the pointer E_1 is left in the stack
(8). Combination now occurs as * > + and + > + so that the
structures E_2 (9) and then E_3 (10) are produced. Finally the stack
is filled once more (11) with the operand d and operator $\dashv$ and
combination (12) produces the final C-structure E_4.

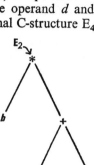

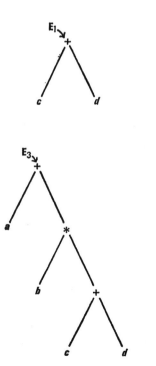

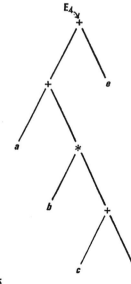

Fig. 7.5

The above example is typical of how a precedence table together with a stack would be used to deal with syntax analysis. There are many variations on this technique but all basically rely on the precedence table for their results.

7.5 Floyd productions

Several compilers and compiler generator systems have used methods similar to one given by Floyd (1961), and these are collectively known as *Floyd productions*. This is an unfortunate misnomer as these methods depend on a matching of part of a sentential form with a preassigned pattern, followed by *reduction* of the sentential form. This method is the basis of the compiler generator systems FSL and CABAL of Carnegie-Mellon University. Parsers using Floyd productions are described by Evans (1964), Feldman (1964), and Pratt and Lindsay (1966).

Algorithms of this type consist of an ordered set of rules for *reducing* the input stream. A special symbol $\triangle$ is used to define a pointer in the input stream and the symbol σ is used to denote any allowable symbol. The rules define rewrite operations on the input stream. An actual implementation usually consists of the symbols to the left of the pointer being stored in a stack and the characters to the right still on the input stream (that is the S-string). Table 7.3 defines a recogniser for the subset of arithmetic expressions introduced in the previous section. The letter I is used to denote the appearance of a member of the class of identifiers. The reduction of the expression $a + b * (c + d) + e$ would then proceed as shown in Table 7.4.

RULE	PRODUCTION		NEXT RULE
1	$(\triangle\,\sigma$	$\Rightarrow (\,\sigma\,\triangle$	1
2	$I\,\triangle\,\sigma$	$\Rightarrow P\,\sigma\,\triangle$	3
3	$T*P\,\sigma\,\triangle$	$\Rightarrow T\,\sigma\,\triangle$	5
4	$P\,\sigma\,\triangle$	$\Rightarrow T\,\sigma\,\triangle$	5
5	$T*\triangle\,\sigma$	$\Rightarrow T*\sigma\,\triangle$	1
6	$E+T\,\sigma\,\triangle$	$\Rightarrow E\,\sigma\,\triangle$	8
7	$T\,\sigma\,\triangle$	$\Rightarrow E\,\sigma\,\triangle$	8
8	$E+\triangle\,\sigma$	$\Rightarrow E+\sigma\,\triangle$	1
9	$(E)\triangle\,\sigma$	$\Rightarrow P\,\sigma\,\triangle$	3
10	$\triangle\,\sigma$	$\Rightarrow \sigma\,\triangle$	1
11	$\vdash E \dashv \triangle$	$\Rightarrow$ exit	

Table 7.3

Rule Applied	Stack after rule applied	Input
		$\triangle\ a + b * (c + d) + e \dashv$
10	$\vdash$ I	$\triangle\ \ \ \ + b * (c + d) + e \dashv$
2	$\vdash$ P $+$	$\triangle\ \ \ \ \ \ b * (c + d) + e \dashv$
4	$\vdash$ T $+$	$\triangle\ \ \ \ \ \ b * (c + d) + e \dashv$
7	$\vdash$ E $+$	$\triangle\ \ \ \ \ \ b * (c + d) + e \dashv$
8	$\vdash$ E $+$ I	$\triangle\ \ \ \ \ \ * (c + d) + e \dashv$
2	$\vdash$ E $+$ P $*$	$\triangle\ \ \ \ \ \ (c + d) + e \dashv$
4	$\vdash$ E $+$ T $*$	$\triangle\ \ \ \ \ \ (c + d) + e \dashv$
5	$\vdash$ E $+$ T $*$ (	$\triangle\ \ \ \ \ \ c + d) + e \dashv$
1	$\vdash$ E $+$ T $*$ (I	$\triangle\ \ \ \ \ \ + d) + e \dashv$
2	$\vdash$ E $+$ T $*$ (P $+$	$\triangle\ \ \ \ \ \ d) + e \dashv$
4	$\vdash$ E $+$ T $*$ (T $+$	$\triangle\ \ \ \ \ \ d) + e \dashv$
7	$\vdash$ E $+$ T $*$ (E $+$	$\triangle\ \ \ \ \ \ d) + e \dashv$
8	$\vdash$ E $+$ T $*$ (E $+$ I	$\triangle\ \ \ \ \ \ ) + e \dashv$
2	$\vdash$ E $+$ T $*$ (E $+$ P)	$\triangle\ \ \ \ \ \ + e \dashv$
4	$\vdash$ E $+$ T $*$ (E $+$ T)	$\triangle\ \ \ \ \ \ + e \dashv$
6	$\vdash$ E $+$ T $*$ (E)	$\triangle\ \ \ \ \ \ + e \dashv$
9	$\vdash$ E $+$ T $*$ P $+$	$\triangle\ \ \ \ \ \ e \dashv$
3	$\vdash$ E $+$ T $+$	$\triangle\ \ \ \ \ \ e \dashv$
6	$\vdash$ E $+$	$\triangle\ \ \ \ \ \ e \dashv$
8	$\vdash$ E $+$ I	$\triangle\ \ \ \ \ \ \dashv$
2	$\vdash$ E $+$ P $\dashv$	$\triangle$
4	$\vdash$ E $+$ T $\dashv$	$\triangle$
6	$\vdash$ E $\dashv$	$\triangle$
11	exit	

Table 7.4

The process is straightforward. It has been assumed that the identifier pointers are transformed into the symbol I on loading into the stack. This is figuratively what might happen. More likely the appearance of I in a rule will be equivalent to causing a check for an identifier pointer to be made on the item in the stack. In Table 7.3, the string of characters to the left of the symbol $\Rightarrow$ defines the stack configuration to be matched, and the string to the right of the symbol defines the symbols to replace the string of characters on the left if a match occurs.

The straightforward algorithm would search the ordered set of rules from the top after each application of a rule until the first rule that could be applied was reached. This would be executed and then the scan would begin at the top again. This tends to be inefficient and the process can be speeded up if an extra column (the final one in Table 7.3) is added which gives the rule to be tried next after the successful application of a rule. The rules are tried sequentially from the point specified until the next rule that is applicable is encountered. This is executed and the *next rule* is then the starting point for the sequential search for the next applicable rule. In the example the number of rules examined without the *next rule* column was 125 compared with 45 when the successor was specified and the initial entry was made at rule 10.

In addition to making the process more efficient it also makes the reductions easier to write. With a continuous set to be scanned from the top at each step, it is vitally important to get the rules in the correct order. With the successor given, rules can be shielded from certain configurations on the input stream and stack so that ordering is not so important. In FSL, a subroutine facility has been added to make recognition of widely used non-terminal symbols easier.

The method allows great flexibility in the form of output, as each recognised rule can have a routine associated with it which defines the required action to be taken on recognition. For example, a postfix string could be output if rule 2 caused the relevant identifier to be output and rules 3 and 6 output * and + respectively. The arithmetic expression in the example would then produce:

$$a\ b\ c\ d + * + e +$$

7.6 Top-down analysis

The top-down analysis method, unlike the methods already described, attempts initially to find the final goal of the analysis. This leads it to look at the sub-goals necessary to achieve the final goal. These sub-goals will involve finding sub-goals and so on. Eventually a sub-goal will require the matching of the input stream with some terminal characters and either this sub-goal is achieved or fails. In the examples given earlier, a notation was defined for producing legal sentences of the language. This same notation can be used as the definition of a recogniser as well as a generator for the language. In the example of English sentences:

$$S \rightarrow P\ Q$$

can be defined as meaning that to recognise the non-terminal symbol S, the non-terminal symbol P must be recognised followed by recognising Q. Analysers which use the syntax definition itself as the data to control the parser are called *syntax directed*.

In the example sentence 'the man has a dog', the top-down process could be described as follows. A *sentence* consists of a *subject phrase* followed by a *verb phrase*. First consider the *subject phrase*. This must consist of 'the' followed by a *noun*. The input stream starts with 'the', so that matches correctly. Will the next part of the input be a *noun*? A *noun* is either the word 'man' or the word 'dog'. The first of these appears next on the input so both 'the' and *noun* have been recognised. Therefore *subject phrase* could be matched with the input string 'the man'. As *sentence* consists of a *subject phrase* followed by a *verb phrase*, can *verb phrase* match the remainder of the input 'has a dog'? The subgoals of *verb phrase* would eventually all be obtained in a similar manner and finally *sentence*, the original goal, would be recognised as *subject phrase* followed by *verb phrase*.

The top-down method described above is called goal-oriented. At each stage a goal is set up. This will in turn involve finding some sub-goals. The sub-goals are checked from left to right and if all are found, the goal itself is found. This goal will usually be a sub-goal itself, and so information that successful recognition has taken place will be passed back to the goal of which this goal is a sub-goal.

The example given above was so trivial that the only place that non-recognition of a goal took place was at the level of the terminal words. However, in general, non-recognition may occur at any level. Alternatively a sub-goal may be able to get recognition in several different ways. The process can then be loosely described as follows:

The initial goal gets recognition from a sub-goal and later gets non-recognition from a second sub-goal. In this case the first sub-goal is repeated to give another alternative recognition if possible and the second sub-goal tried again. This continual back-tracking to try and find alternative sub-goals on failure makes the algorithm quite complex and also slow when implemented. An excellent description of such an algorithm is given by Floyd (1964). A simple example requiring the need to back-track once a reasonable sub-goal has been found is as follows:

$$S \rightarrow A \; x$$
$$A \rightarrow v$$
$$A \rightarrow B$$
$$B \rightarrow v \; w$$

where the input is 'v w x '.

To recognise S, the sub-goal A must first be recognised. Taking the first rule involving A, the character 'v' is matched and the sub-goal A recognised. To recognise S, the character 'x' must match the remainder of the input stream 'w x'. This fails and so the sub-goal A must be attempted again. This time the string 'v w' is recognised as B and then A. The goal S is then recognised by the final matching of 'x'.

The algorithm described above has been given the name *slow-back*. A more efficient but less general top-down analyser is called a *fast-back*. The difference between the two algorithms is that, in the fast-back, once a sub-goal has been recognised, the assumption is made that this recognition is the correct one and the original goal, if it fails when attempting a later sub-goal, will immediately return with non-recognition rather than attempt to find alternative recognitions of the first sub-goal. As well as being much more efficient, the fast-back is simpler to construct than the slow-back. The problem of keeping information about sub-goals already entered and returned from is now removed. Only information about partially recognised goals need be kept. As most computer languages can have their syntax specified in a form that can be recognised by a fast-back, the slow-back has not been used to any extent in compilers. Examples of fast-back top-down analysers can be found in Glennie (1960); Brooker, Morris and Rohl (1962); Cheatham and Sattley (1964); and Banerji (1966).

One problem with top-down parsers is their inability to deal with left-recursion in a language. Consider, for example, the rule:

$$E \rightarrow E + T$$

in the definition of an arithmetic expression. If this was presented to a top-down parser, then to recognise E it is necessary to recognise the sub-goals E, '+' and T. Consider the first sub-goal E. To recognise the sub-goal E, the sub-goals E, '+' and T must be recognised, and so on. This process obviously goes on indefinitely. The problem of left-recursion can either be solved by changing the original set of rules defining the language or by having the parser itself do this rearrangement. Changing the rules will often change the syntactic structure itself however. For example:

$$E \rightarrow E + T$$
$$E \rightarrow T$$

could be replaced by

$$E \rightarrow T X$$
$$X \rightarrow +T X$$
$$X \rightarrow \Lambda$$

Descriptions of top-down fast-back parsers handling left-recursion can be found in Cheatham (1966) and Banerji (1966).

The other major problem, which is usually easier to solve, is the order in which the rules are written. As these are tried in sequential order for a particular non-terminal, it is important that a rule which is part of a larger rule comes after the larger rule. Consider:

$$E \rightarrow B$$
$$E \rightarrow B C$$

When presented in that order, recognition would always be achieved on the first before attempting the second, so that the second rule would never be tried. In this case they must be ordered the other way around. In addition, the efficiency of the algorithm can be improved if rules having the same *stems* are grouped together. For example:

$$E \to B\ a$$
$$E \to B\ b$$

would, as it stands, cause the first rule to recognise B and then, if failure occurs on the match with 'a', would try the next rule. The next rule would enter and recognise B again before recognising 'b'. If the rules are grouped together, then the algorithm can be made to only recognise B once and, if failure to match 'a' occurs, then it tries immediately to match 'b'. An example of such an algorithm is given in Brooker, Morris and Rohl (1962).

7.6.1 *Selective top-down analysis*

In the example English sentence, the top-down analyser would first attempt to recognise the *subject phrase*. This in its turn required 'the' followed by a *noun* to be found as sub-goals. To stop the searching of fruitless paths, one modification, which has been applied, is to deduce beforehand what are the possible words that can start any phrase and, before attempting a sub-goal, to check that the characters on the input stream do satisfy this condition. This could of course in some cases lead to a considerable saving in time spent in searching for false goals.

In the example, the following relations could be set up:

⟨sentence⟩	the
⟨subject phrase⟩	the
⟨verb phrase⟩	has
⟨object phrase⟩	a, the

where the right hand column defines the words which could start the non-terminal symbol. Before attempting to check any of these phrases the input stream would first be checked to ensure that it commences with the correct word. This analysis could obviously be carried further. The first two possible words could be stored or, going to the extreme, all legal sentences in the language could be stored. Obviously the latter would be very inefficient and somewhere in between there is an optimum strategy. This depends on the language concerned and it is difficult to generalise. Typically, a single character has been used. With each phrase is stored an ordered set of bits equal in number to the number of terminal symbols. Each bit represents whether or not a particular terminal symbol can appear at the head of the phrase. The improvement in performance of a selective top-down is offset by the inflexibility built into the parser. With a straightforward top-down it is a simple matter to change definitions as required. Conversely in a selective top-down, such changes will require the updating of all the bits dependent on the phrase replaced. This may well be as complex as the original setting up of the *selection bits*.

The paper by Brooker (1967) implies that, in the language of the Compiler-Compiler, selective top-down gave no appreciable improvement over top-down.

7.7 Bottom-up analysis

Considering the English sentence 'the man has a dog' once again, the parsing algorithm might have proceeded as follows. The goal is to produce the non-terminal ⟨sentence⟩. First consider the possible rules to see if a rule exists which starts with the word 'the'. There are two of these:

$$⟨article⟩ \qquad → the$$
$$⟨subject\ phrase⟩ \qquad → the\ ⟨noun⟩$$

Considering the first, the sentential form is now:

$$⟨article⟩\ man\ has\ a\ dog$$

The only rule starting with ⟨article⟩ is ⟨object phrase⟩. However, ⟨object phrase⟩ is not completed yet so, instead of continuing to aim for the goal, ⟨sentence⟩, this could be stored and a new goal ⟨noun⟩ set up to match the input string 'man has a dog'. The non-terminal ⟨noun⟩ *is* recognised and so therefore is ⟨object phrase⟩. The sentential form is now:

$$⟨object\ phrase⟩\ has\ a\ dog$$

and the original goal, ⟨sentence⟩, is required once more. However, no rules start with ⟨object phrase⟩ and so this parse is incorrect. Back tracking, the second rule is tried starting with 'the'. This will require the remainder of ⟨subject phrase⟩ to be recognised as a sub-goal before proceeding. Once ⟨noun⟩ has been recognised, ⟨subject phrase⟩ has been recognised. In order to recognise ⟨sentence⟩, therefore, the sentential form 'has a dog' must be recognised as a ⟨verb phrase⟩. Once again the parsing is done by starting at the terminal symbols and seeing which rules start with 'has'. A hypothetical ⟨verb phrase⟩ will eventually be built up from the terminal symbols, and finally the original goal ⟨sentence⟩ will be achieved. At each stage a goal is set up and a parsing is attempted by examining a sentential form to see if the goal can be reached from the sentential form.

The parse of the arithmetic expression $a + b * c$ is shown diagrammatically in Fig. 7.6. The letter g is used to point at the current goal and the letter i points to the start of the sentential form from which this goal is hoped to be obtained initially. The pointer i is moved along the sentential form as sub-goals of the goal g are recognised.

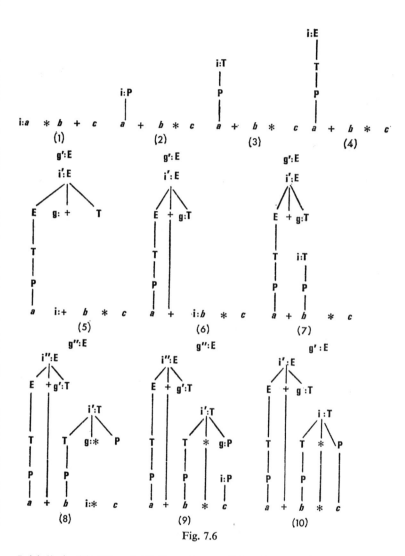

Fig. 7.6

Initially in (1), (2) and (3) the only possible rules are obeyed. At this stage either the rule E → T or T → T * P could be applied. Assume the first is chosen (4); there is now a match between the goal E and the structure produced so far. However the input is not exhausted, therefore E → E + T must be used (5). At this stage an uncompleted

61

structure defining E has been produced. The current goal could still be aimed for at this point and the match between the structure produced and the goal made. However, if the canonical parse is required, then it is best to stack the current pointer and goal (denoted by g' and i') and to set up a subsidiary goal. This goal is the leftmost uncompleted part of the structure and a subsidiary pointer which points to the leftmost completed structure. In (5), i points to '+' on the input stream and g points to the '+' in the structure. As the structure '+' is complete (it is just a symbol on the input stream), a match occurs. The next goal to choose is again the leftmost one of the uncompleted structure. Diagrams (6), (7) and (8) show how the structure to this goal is made. At this point the structure T is not complete and the current goal must be stacked again and a subsidiary goal set up. In (9) the subsidiary goal is completed and the previous goal and pointer are unstacked (10). As T is now complete, this structure can be matched and the original goal reset. This again will be matched and the complete structure produced.

The parser which chooses to deal with leftmost uncompleted subgoals first, as described above, is called *left corner bottom-up*. The algorithm can be modified to be *selective* by again forming a table which gives the possible terminal or non-terminal symbols that can start any goal. This check can then be made each time either a new goal or pointer position is defined. This stops the processing of a large number of incorrect goals.

Mixed top-down and bottom-up strategies have been used. For example, at (6) in the above example it would have been possible to change to a top-down parser to complete the subtree before continuing. This hybrid approach can be used to keep down the number of stacked goals. Descriptions of bottom-up analysers are given by Cheatham and Sattley (1964) and Ingermann (1966).

7.8 Comparison of parsers

Unquestionably, the most efficient of the parsers described is the one using operator precedence. The advantages are that only a subset (the operators) of the total input need be examined when generating the structure and that no back tracking occurs. Its disadvantage is that it may require a more complex lexical pass to get the S-string in the desired form and some languages may not be processed at all by this method. However, with languages in current use, it is still probably the most useful of the parsing algorithms.

The methods using Floyd productions can be hand tuned to give fairly efficient recognition. However, this will depend on how quickly a production can be matched and how long the path is before the next correct production is reached.

Top-down and bottom-up parsers have been compared by Griffiths and Petrick (1965). The results were, however, inconclusive because of the artificial languages considered and the method of defining the top-down parser. It is not obvious at present which is the more useful for computer languages in use today.

7.9 Implementation of operator precedence parsers

The operator precedence method was described briefly in Section 7.3. The decision on whether to fill the stack or produce some combination of the stack elements was made by examining a precedence table. As can be seen from Fig. 7.3, there are only four possible entries in the precedence table. It can contain one of the operations $<$, $>$, $\doteq$ or it may be empty. An empty entry implies that in the language there are two operators that should never appear next to each other. As there are only four possibilities, these can be stored in two binary digits so that the amount of space used by the precedence table is very small. The two bits could be stored together in a two-dimensional table. The drawbacks of such an arrangement in practice are that the action to be taken at each entry must be fairly rigid, combination must occur in a set manner and no special operations on the stack can be introduced.

The alternative is to have each entry in the precedence table containing a pointer to a routine to be executed when the relevant pair of operators appear on the top of the stack. This allows housekeeping and non-standard actions to be done, for example, by the routines when special stack configurations are encountered. Consider, for example, a compiler for a statement such as:

$$\textbf{real } a, b, c;$$

The identifiers will have been entered in the symbol table by the lexical scan and the pointer to this entry would appear in the S-string. The operator **real** would be a single symbol. The stacking would proceed as shown in Fig. 7.7. In this example, the operation defined for (**real**, ',') would be a special routine which would mark the position of the identifier in the symbol table as being of type **real** and then remove the top operand and operator from the stack before filling. The (**real**, ;) position would again make an entry in the dictionary followed by removal of the top *two* operators, and filling.

Another useful operation would be to change the operators in the stack itself when a small routine is executed. This allows the action

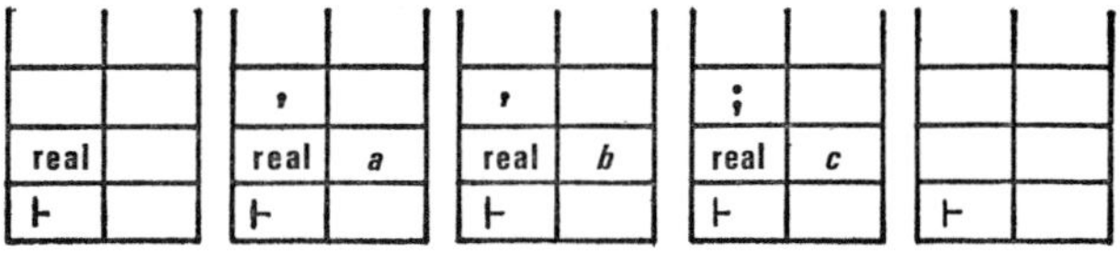

Fig. 7.7

63

required in certain positions to be varied depending on previous context. It allows parsing of languages which are, in theory, not operator precedence grammars. It is rather similar to the transformations produced on the stack by the Floyd productions method.

The use of a bit table for the precedence table means that only decisions such as fill or combine are allowed on the stack. A more flexible combination action can be obtained if combination is always assumed to be between an operator and two operands. This means that the $\doteq$ operator is only allowed to apply between bracketing symbols such as (and) which can be treated specially. In Fig. 7.4, position (6) could cause the expression E_1 to be moved to the free operand position on the stack level containing *, followed by the reading of the next operator into the stack. The operator $\doteq$ can then be thought of as a special form of combination. If this is done, then each combination occurs between a particular operator and operands. Each can be treated differently by having an *operator table* which specifies the desired action. Being one-dimensional this is obviously more conservative on space than the two-dimensional precedence table containing pointers.

It may be that the action required for several different operators is the same as far as the precedence table is concerned. For example, $+$ and $-$ can be considered the same as far as their syntactic relationship with other operators is concerned. In this case it may be reasonable to consider the precedence table entries as being defined by *operator classes* rather than operators. The stack could be increased to give columns for both the operator and operator class and the switching will be done on the classes. The lexical scan could easily be designed to provide both these symbols on the S-string.

For precedence tables, it is possible that two *precedence functions*, f and g, can be defined so that if $X < Y$ then $f(X) < g(Y)$, if $X \doteq Y$ then $f(X) = g(Y)$ and if $X > Y$ then $f(X) > g(Y)$. A table giving values of f and g for the various operators might be more compact, although it is not completely obvious. Given the precedence table, a method for defining precedence functions, if they exist, is described by Floyd (1963). Floyd defines a precedence table and functions for Algol. The size of the precedence table was 34 by 35 which would require 2380 bits compared with the precedence functions which required 5 bits each and therefore 345 bits. This difference is not large and the precedence functions do not give any means of defining error positions. In an actual implementation this difference in storage size may well be even less, so that it is not too obvious how useful precedence functions are in practice.

8

CODE GENERATION FOR ARITHMETIC EXPRESSIONS

8.1 Introduction

One of the major problems in the compilation of scientific languages is the production of efficient object code for arithmetic assignment statements in a reasonable compilation time. For example, the relative efficiency of two Fortran compilers in the execution of a program will depend almost entirely on the code produced for arithmetic statements. The term *arithmetic statement* is used here to include those statements which have evaluation of arithmetic expressions as part of the statement. For example the Fortran statement:

IF (A + B*C + D) 10,11,12

is equivalent to:

T = A + B*C + D
IF (T) 10,11,12

where T is some temporary storage (possibly the accumulator) allocated by the compiler. In this example, coding the assignment statement will be considered as part of the problem, while the simplified IF statement will not. Similarly:

      DO 10 I = 1,5
10   A(I,J) = B(I,J) + C(K,J)

where A,B,C, are 10 by 10 arrays, is equivalent to:

      I = 1
1   L = 10*J + I + A − 11
      M = 10*J + I + B − 11
      N = 10*J + K + C − 11
      a(L) = a(M) + a(N)
      I = I + 1
      IF (I − 5) 1,1,2
2   CONTINUE

where A,B,C represent the base addresses of the arrays and the function 'a' is used to imply that the statement means 'add the contents of location M to the contents of location N and store in location L'. Here, all but the IF statement will be treated as arithmetic.

Optimisation of the code produced for arithmetic statements is usually criticised for being wasteful of compilation time. The criticism is that finding common sub-expressions and eliminating the excessive use of temporary storage, etc. could be done by the programmer and is therefore not the duty of the compiler writer. This argument might be reasonable if only the actual arithmetic assignment statements were being considered. However, in the augmented set, most languages do *not* allow the programmer to aid the optimisation of the code produced. The user is *not* able to point out the similarity between the addressing functions for A(I,J) and B(I,J) for example.

This chapter should therefore be considered as dealing with the arithmetic part of all statement types in the language rather than the simple assignment statement.

8.2 A hypothetical computer

The production of good object code depends to a large extent on the computer concerned. It is difficult to consider this question without having a specific computer in mind. Consequently, a hypothetical computer will be defined which has an order code sufficiently resembling those of genuine computers so that the strategies outlined in this chapter can be easily seen to be applicable fairly generally.

The hypothetical computer will be assumed to have a single accumulator. The order code will be assumed to contain both normalised and unnormalised floating point operations. Numbers will be assumed to be stored in the form $b*10^i$ where i is an integer and b is a three-figure decimal fraction between 0 and 1. In the normalised form, the leading digit of the mantissa is not zero. For example, the normalised form of 5 is $\cdot500*10^1$, not $\cdot050*10^2$ or $\cdot005*10^3$. REAL variables will be stored as normalised floating point numbers. INTEGER variables will be stored with a fixed exponent of 3. Thus a variable having the value 57 would be stored as $\cdot057*10^3$ if it was INTEGER, but $\cdot570*10^2$ if it was REAL.

The order code consists of the six basic orders:

L	Load accumulator from storage location.
ADD	Add contents of storage location to accumulator.
SUB	Subtract contents of storage location from accumulator.
MPY	Multiply accumulator by contents of storage location.
DIV	Divide accumulator by contents of storage location.
ST	Set contents of storage location equal to accumulator.

These orders may produce a result which is either normalised or unnormalised, depending on whether the letter U or N follows the mnemonic. In the case of a normalised result, the exponent is adjusted until the first digit after the decimal point is non-zero. To do an unnormalised addition or subtraction, the smaller exponent is first made equal to the larger by adjusting the mantissa and then the operation takes place. For example adding $\cdot003*10^3$ to $\cdot270*10^2$ will produce $\cdot030*10^3$. Adding $\cdot750*10^2$ to $\cdot000*10^3$ would produce $\cdot075*10^3$. This could be used, therefore, as a means for producing the standard unnormalised form for INTEGER numbers.

The absolute value of the quantity being taken from, or set into, a store location will be used if the mnemonic has the letter A added at the end of the load or store instruction. Some examples of code generated for expressions involving the INTEGER variables I,J,K and REAL variables B,C,D are as follows:

1    $I + J$ LU I,   ADDU J
2    $D = ABS(B - C)$ LN B,   SUBN C,   STNA D

Notice that STUA would also have been correct here as the previous order has already produced a normalised result.

3    $D = B*I$ LN B,   MPYN I,   STN D
4    $J = B$ LN B,   FIX   ,   STU J

The operation FIX is defined as the set of orders required which will change the normalised form of the accumulator to the standard unnormalised INTEGER representation. It could be, for example, the operation ADDU $0*10^3$. This is an important operation and will be left as FIX as this may be quite different on different computers. The assumption will be that it requires the use of the accumulator.

5    $I = J*I$ LU J,   MPYN I,   FIX,   STU I
6    $I = J*I + K$ LU J,   MPYN I,   ADDU K,   STU I

Notice that the addition of K is sufficient to force the result into the standard INTEGER form so that FIX is not required.

These examples give some indication of the variety of code required for special purposes. An abbreviated form of the mnemonic will be used without the relevant N,U qualifier if it is either irrelevant or obvious which should be used.

8.3 An elementary algorithm using an operator table

In Section 7.4 an algorithm was defined for parsing an operator precedence grammar. In Section 7.9 a slightly modified algorithm was given which used an *operator table* to define any special action required for a particular operator when it was involved in combination defined by the Precedence Table. This operator table could be used to produce code directly a combination occurs. In this case, there is no need to produce a tree representation of the expression as was done in Fig. 7.5. The contents of the accumulator will now be loosely equivalent to the tree pointers E_i produced in Fig. 7.4. The operand position of the stack will be set to contain either the address of the variable in that position or alternatively a special marker denoting the address of the accumulator. If it is necessary to store the contents of the accumulator in a working space during the evaluation, then this will be done by generating the code ST *TEMP*. The effect on the stack will be to replace the special marker denoting *ACC* by the location of the temporary variable. This then behaves like any other variable. The allocation of temporary storage will not be dealt with at this point.

On combination, code will be produced dependent on the top two operands and their infix operator. As this will result in the value of the expression being set in the accumulator, the operand position, where previously the tree pointer E_i would be set, now will contain the special marker *ACC*. At each combination, the possibilities are that one or both of the operands may be variables (denoted by *V*) and one may be the accumulator (denoted by *ACC*). Using *TOS* to represent the top operand of the stack, *TOSM* to represent the next lower operand of the stack and OP to represent the infix operator involved in the combination, then the code generated is as follows:

1. If any operand position lower than *TOSM* in the stask contains the marker *ACC* then produce code

ST *TEMP*

and change position in operand stack containing *ACC* to the address of the temporary storage.

2. Produce code as follows:

TOSM	OP	*TOS*	CODE PRODUCED
V_1	$+-/*$	V_2	L V_1, OP V_2
ACC	$+-/*$	*V*	OP *V*
V	$+*$	*ACC*	OP *V*
V	$-/$	*ACC*	ST *TEMP*, L *V*, OP *TEMP*

OP is defined as the mnemonic ADD, SUB, DIV, MPY depending on which of $+, -, /, *$ is equal to OP. The stacking and code generation at each stage is shown in Fig. 8.1 for the expression $a*b/(c + d)$.

The combination caused by the relation $+ >)$ causes the *ACC* to be stored by rule 1 while the *V*/*ACC* causes the other temporary storage. The first storage into temporary workspace was caused by a partially evaluated expression being followed by a sub-expression in brackets which required the use of the accumulator. The second

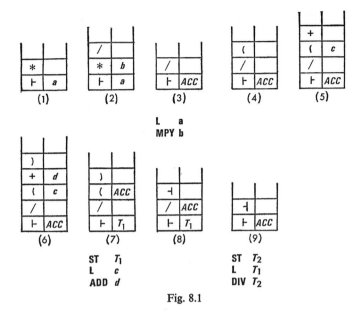

Fig. 8.1

storage into workspace is required because the defined order code of the computer does not have the *reverse divide* operation:

'Set Accumulator equal to contents of storage location divided by accumulator'

In many cases these stores into temporary working spaces can be eliminated by delaying the code production until more information about the complete arithmetic expression is available.

8.4 An algorithm for generating code from a tree structure

In Section 7.4 a parser for an operator precedence grammar was defined which produced a binary tree as a C-structure. An example of the type of tree produced was given in Fig. 7.5. The tree structure consists of a set of nodes and at each node is situated an operator. Each node has two pointers (left and right) which point either to terminal identifiers or lower nodes of the tree. These will be called the left and right operand of the tree node. For each node, T, is defined:

OP.T   the operator of node T
L.T   the left hand operand of node T
R.T   the right hand operand of node T

In the notation in Section 8.3, combination produces the following action:

69

1 OP.T = operator concerned in combination
2 L.T = *TOSM*
3 R.T = *TOS*
4 *TOSM* = T
5 Move stack pointer down one level

The expression $(a + b*c)/(f*g - (d + e)/(h + k))$ would, for example, produce the tree shown in Fig. 8.2. The circled numbers indicate the order in which the tree nodes are produced by the syntax analysis when generating the C-structure. A routine for producing code equivalent to the tree T could be defined as C(T). In the example, the node marked as 8 is the *root* of the tree and so C(8) defines the code required to evaluate the expression. The operation C(T) will be defined as one which generates code equivalent to the whole tree with T as root and, if this is a sub-tree of the whole C-structure, it will replace the sub-tree T in the structure by the special terminal symbol *ACC*. This symbol denotes that at this stage in the coding the value of the sub-tree is resident in the accumulator.

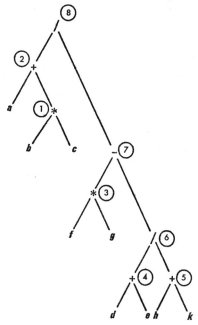

Fig. 8.2

The action required when attempting to generate code for a node T will depend on the operator OP.T and whether the two sub-trees, L.T and R.T, consist of a variable, a node or the special symbol *ACC*. Therefore, a three by three table is required for each operator denoting the action to be taken for each possibility. Of course, several operators will have identical tables and, for the hypothetical order code given, only two tables are required (one for $+,*$ and the other for $-,/$). These are given in Table 8.1. As before, temporary storage is made available as required and can then be treated in the same way as any other variable. The tables have been written out in their simplest form. In an actual implementation it is quite likely that

OP.T = $+,*$	Variable V_2	Node	ACC
Variable V_1	L V_1 OP V_2 T = ACC	C(R.T) C(T)	OP V_1 T = ACC
Node	C(L.T) C(T)	Either C(R.T) C(T) or C(L.T) C(T)	ST TEMP R.T = TEMP C(T)
ACC	OP V_2 T = ACC	ST TEMP L.T = TEMP C(T)	Illegal

OP.T = $-,/$	Variable V_2	Node	ACC
Variable V_1	L V_1 OP V_2 T = ACC	C(R.T) C(T)	ST TEMP R.T = TEMP C(T)
Node	C(L.T) C(T)	C(R.T) C(T)	ST TEMP R.T = TEMP C(T)
ACC	OP V_2 T = ACC	Illegal	Illegal

Table 8.1

some short cuts will be taken. For example, the (NODE, *ACC*) entry in the tables requires the accumulator to be stored, the left hand sub-tree to be coded, and then the (ACC,V) code to be produced. In the table this appears as generating the 'accumulator to storage' instruction followed by re-entering the routine to code the new form of T which is now of the form (NODE,V). In practice, all the code required, other than the coding of the left node, would be defined at the (NODE,*ACC*) table entry rather than re-entering as given in the table. The main difference in the two tables is due to the order code lacking the 'reverse divide' and 'negate and add' instructions. Consequently, if the node T has two sub-trees, then for addition and multiplication it does not matter which sub-tree is coded first, whereas it is important to code the right sub-tree first for subtraction and division, as this may avoid some unnecessary temporary storages.

The example given in Fig. 8.2 would be coded as follows:

(a) $C(8)$. As both L.8 and R.8 are nodes, the action is given in the (NODE,NODE) entry for the operator division. This is $C(7)$ followed by $C(8)$.

(b) $C(7)$. Again the (NODE,NODE) entry is required. This is $C(6)$ followed by $C(7)$.

(c) $C(6)$. Again the (NODE,NODE) entry is required. This is $C(5)$ followed by $C(6)$.

(d) $C(5)$. Both L.5 and R.5 are variables. The (V,V) entry produces code:

$$\text{L} \quad h$$
$$\text{ADD} \quad k$$

leaving ACC in place of node 5.

(e) Completing (c) above requires $C(6)$ to be coded next. This now has R.6 equal to ACC. The (NODE,ACC) entry generates the code:

$$\text{ST} \quad TEMP$$

and replaces ACC by the variable $TEMP$ and then re-enters to generate $C(6)$.

(f) $C(6)$ is now (NODE,V) and requires $C(4)$, the left hand sub-tree, followed by $C(6)$.

(g) $C(4)$ like (d) produces:

$$\text{L} \quad d$$
$$\text{ADD} \quad e$$

(h) As (g) leaves ACC in place of node 4, the form of 6 is now (ACC,V) and the code

$$\text{DIV} \quad TEMP$$

is generated and node 6 replaced by ACC

(i) $C(7)$ must now be coded etc.

The complete code produced using the tree structure is compared with the code produced using the elementary algorithm in Table 8.2. By leaving code generation until the complete C-structure is available three store and three load instructions have been removed and, in addition, the number of temporary storage locations used could be reduced from four to one if the allocation scheme for temporary storage feels it is desirable.

$$(a + b*c)/(f*g - (d + e)/(h + k))$$

ELEMENTARY ALGORITHM		TREE ALGORITHM	
L	b	L	h
MPY	c	ADD	k
ADD	a	ST	T_1
ST	T_1	L	d
L	f	ADD	e
MPY	g	DIV	T_1
ST	T_2	ST	T_1
L	d	L	f
ADD	e	MPY	g
ST	T_3	SUB	T_1
L	h	ST	T_1
ADD	k	L	b
ST	T_4	MPY	c
L	T_3	ADD	a
DIV	T_4	DIV	T_1
ST	T_3		
L	T_2		
SUB	T_3		
ST	T_2		
L	T_1		
DIV	T_2		

Table 8.2

The unnecessary stores generated by an expression of the form $a*b*(c + d)$ have not been removed. The tree algorithm is required to code a tree consisting of the second * as the root operator. In this (NODE,NODE) situation for producing code, the entry gave two alternatives and, without further analysis, it would be unable to decide which was preferable. In the example, obviously it is preferable to code the right sub-tree, $c + d$, first. A simple exploration of the tree would have solved this particular case but, in general, it is usually better to attempt to solve the problem before the tree is constructed. The problem arises because the $a*b$ is generated as a tree before the sub-expression $c + d$ appears in the stack. With a string of operands connected by operators with the same precedence class (often called a *segment*) there is no reason why these have to be combined as soon as they appear in the stack. The relationship $* > *$, $* > /$, $+ > +$ etc. cause this immediate combination. If these relations were changed to $\doteq$, then operators of the same class would fill the stack until the complete segment was available when an operator of a different class would cause combination of the whole segment. An expression $a*b*c*d$, for example, instead of having a

73

fixed structure $(((a*b)*c)*d)$, would defer the decision on structure until the whole segment had been loaded into the stack. A simple algorithm for improving the code generated is to sort the operands so that combination occurs between the non-terminal expressions first followed by the terminals. This could be achieved in the stack by re-ordering the operands so that the highest operands in the stack are the non-terminal expressions and then combining from the top of the stack to form the tree. The expression $a*b*(c + d)*e$ would then, in effect, have the structure $(a*(b*(e*(c + d))))$.

8.5 More complex algorithms

More sophisticated algorithms than those described above have been used to deal with the problems of long segments of operands combined by operators of the same precedence class. These usually involve defining the C-structure in a more fluid form so that rearrangements can be made easily.

An example of such a structure is the one used in the early Fortran compilers and defined by Sheridan (1959). Basically, the C-structure consists of a set of *triples*, written (N,OP,D) where N is a number given to the segment, and OP is the operator defined on the variable D. D can either be a variable or a segment number defining a sub-expression. The expression $a*b*(c + d)*e$ would produce the triples $(0,*,a)$, $(0,*,b)$, $(0,*,1)$, $(0,*,e)$, $(1,+,c)$, $(1,+,d)$. The advantage of the method is the flexibility of the structure. For example, the individual elements of a segment can be easily reordered. However, production of good code requires quite a large amount of sorting and rearranging of triples. Consequently it is much slower than the simpler tree algorithm.

Other coding algorithms of interest are given by Hawkins and Huxtable (1963); Kanner, Kosinski and Robinson (1965); Randell and Russell (1964); and Graham (1964). Details of a tree algorithm similar to that defined in the previous section are given by Anderson (1965). A modified form of this for a computer with several accumulators is given by Nakata (1967).

8.6 Unary operators and transfer functions

A *unary* operator is one having only one operand. This is in contrast to $*,/$ etc. which are binary operators. The most common unary operator is the unary minus in, for example, $(-a)*b$. The hypothetical order code defined in Section 8.2 allows the load and store instructions to be modified so that the absolute value of the operand can be used if the mnemonic has an A inserted at the end. This modification could be made use of in the type of code generated, and consequently the function ABS should be treated as a special unary. In some computer order codes most of the standard functions such as SIN, COS etc. have special computer instructions associated with them so that again these can be treated specially. The functions to be treated as unary operators will depend entirely on the order code and the sophistication of output code required. The problems of code generation often arise from the inconsistencies of the order code. In the hypothetical order code, the 'reverse divide' and 'negate and add' instructions were missing. Similarly, the absolute value of the operand could be taken only in the load and store instructions.

In the example, arithmetic operations were either normalised or unnormalised. Because of the representation of INTEGER quantities chosen, a number may be changed from INTEGER form to REAL form by simply performing some normalised operation on the number. This *transfer function*, changing the mode of the number from INTEGER to REAL, will be called the mode transfer function R (this is equivalent to the Fortran function FLOAT). Similarly the transfer function, which produces the integer part of a REAL number as an INTEGER, will be given the name I (equivalent to the Fortran function FIX). Again, problems will arise because one transfer function R is simple to produce and often requires no additional instructions (its effect can be amalgamated with one of the arithmetic operations) whereas the transfer function I may be more difficult to produce and require additional instructions. In this case, it is important to avoid any unnecessary transfers to the mode INTEGER. For example, in Algol, the arithmetic expression $(i*j + k*m)*a$ is of mode REAL where i,j,k,m are INTEGER and 'a' is REAL. The sub-expressions $i*j$ and $k*m$ are of mode INTEGER. One of these must be calculated and stored in working space on a computer with only one accumulator. In a simple approach, as this expression is of mode INTEGER and as the multiplication will have resulted in a normalised floating point number, a transfer function I must be applied before storing in the workspace. However, as a more detailed analysis would show that the final result is of mode REAL, the transfer function is not required. The problem could be further complicated by the sub-expression appearing elsewhere in a position where it was important that the expression was of mode INTEGER. In this case the transfer function *would* be necessary. These are the kinds of problems facing the code generator.

During the code production, the contents of the accumulator or store location can be in one of three modes:

- F   Normalised floating point
- S   Unnormalised floating point
- M   Normalised floating point integer (obtained when multiplying two INTEGER quantities)

Similarly arithmetic expressions can have one of the following sign functions operating on them:

1 $+$
2 $-$
3 ABS
4 $-ABS$

8.6.1 *Defining code during stack combination*

In the simple algorithm defined in Section 8.3, code is generated as the stack is combined. Therefore, the particular form of the code required must also be defined at this point. In the other algorithms described, the code is generated from the C-structure and so details of whether the code should be normalised or unnormalised could be left until then, or alternatively this may be decided at the formation of the C-structure.

The simplest method of keeping the additional information required is to have two additional columns in the stack. The first defines the mode of the operand and the second defines the sign function still to be applied to the result. The aim will be to keep the mode produced as close to the desired mode as possible without generating additional instructions, and similarly attempt to keep the sign function to $+$. It may be necessary to have a third column defining the mode required of the result. This would either be INTEGER or REAL in the example.

In the simple algorithm defined in Section 8.3, there was only one possible action for each of the different combinations of TOSM,OP and TOS. This action would now be expanded to a four by four table depending on the sign function to be applied to *TOSM* and *TOS*. The action required for different operators will be quite different now. A table for the operator * and the case where operands *TOSM* and *TOS* are both variables and not *ACC* is given as an example in Table 8.3. Apart from the code to be generated, each entry contains the sign function acting on the result. Notice that the *ABS,ABS* entry would require four instructions to generate the correct code including the sign:

$$
\begin{array}{ll}
\text{LA} & V_1 \\
\text{ST} & TEMP \\
\text{LA} & V_2 \\
\text{MPY} & TEMP
\end{array}
$$

In the hope that this can be avoided at a later stage, the equality $ABS(a*b) = ABS(a)*ABS(b)$ is used to leave the function ABS operating on the result. Similar tables for the other operators are required. Stacking and code generation for the expression:

$$ABS(a* - b + c*ABS(d))*ABS(e)$$

is shown in Fig. 8.3. The complete stacking and combination is shown for the first *ABS*. The stages showing combination for the other occurrences have been omitted. The first rule of the algorithm which stores the accumulator in temporary workspace would, of

OP = *	+	-	ABS	-ABS
+	L V_1 MPY V_2 +	L V_1 MPY V_2 -	LA V_2 MPY V_1 +	LA V_2 MPY V_1 -
-	L V_1 MPY V_2 -	L V_1 MPY V_2 +	LA V_2 MPY V_1 -	LA V_2 MPY V_1 +
ABS	LA V_1 MPY V_2 +	LA V_1 MPY V_2 -	L V_1 MPY V_2 ABS	L V_1 MPY V_2 -ABS
-ABS	LA V_1 MPY V_2 -	LA V_1 MPY V_2 +	L V_1 MPY V_2 -ABS	L V_1 MPY V_2 ABS

Table 8.3

course, be modified to take account of any *ABS* function operating on the accumulator. In this case STA instead of ST would be used, and the *ABS* part of the sign function removed.

The fourth column which defines the mode would be used to indicate whether a normalised or unnormalised operation is required. In this case, the following tables would indicate the type of operation

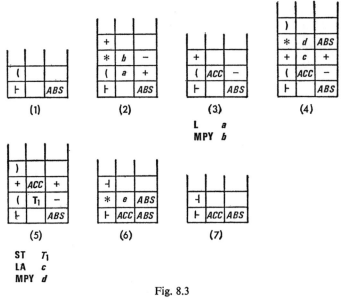

Fig. 8.3

77

required where one operand is a variable and the other the accumulator.

+	F	S	M		*	F	S	M
F	NF	NF	NF		F	NF	NF	NF
S	NF	US	US		S	NF	NM	NM
M	NF	US	NM		M	NF	NM	NM

The first letter in the table defines whether the code generated is to be normalised (N) or unnormalised (U) and the second defines the mode of the result. Notice that in the addition table, an unnormalised operation can force the result back to integer mode if the original mode was M. This would happen in generating code for $i*j + k$ where all the variables are INTEGER.

This method does not deal with the mode transfer operators very well. The table for + could be altered, for example, if a REAL result was wanted so that the S,S entry was a normalised operation. However, as before, more details of the whole C-structure are required to get efficient code for mode transfer functions.

8.6.2 *Unary operators in the tree algorithm*

In this approach the operators R, I, ABS, and unary minus are left as part of the C-structure. They appear in the tree as nodes with only one operand. They can be thought of as modifying the binary node or terminal below. Any implicit mode changes in the arithmetic expression can also be inserted as explicit unary operators in this manner. The *mode transfer function* (MTF) is defined as the total effect of all modal functions on the node below, and similarly the *sign transfer function* (STF) is the total effect of the sign unaries on the node.

The sub-trees L.T and R.T are now terminal if the MTF operating on the terminal is still terminal, and similarly for STF. As shown before the operator I, which takes the integral part, may well use the accumulator when acting upon a REAL quantity. Therefore this would not be terminal.

As coding of the tree takes place, the accumulator and temporary storages will contain quantities which resemble what is actually wanted at each point in the coding of the tree. If it is impossible to produce the exact form in the minimum number of orders, then the difference is passed up the tree in the hope that, at a higher level, the actual contents of the accumulator agrees with what is wanted. There are seven different mode transfer functions that will arise. The definitions given here are in terms of the accumulator but also apply for storage locations.

S the accumulator contains an unnormalised integer and this is required.

F the accumulator contains a normalised floating point number and this is required.

IM the accumulator contains a normalised floating point number which is an integer and eventually this is required to be an INTEGER in unnormalised form.

RM the accumulator contains a normalised floating point number which is an integer and eventually this is required to be a REAL number.

RS the accumulator contains an unnormalised integer which is eventually required to be a REAL number and therefore normalised.

IF the accumulator contains a normalised floating point number and an INTEGER number equal to the integral part of this is required eventually.

RIF the accumulator contains a normalised floating point number and a REAL number, equal to the integral part of this, is required eventually.

This notation is slightly ambiguous as S,F are used both to represent the mode of a variable and also the null transfer function operating on a variable of that mode. The transfer functions I and R have been subdivided into classes depending on the particular form of the accumulator or storage location. Starting at the lower node, L.T or R.T, each transfer function can be applied to the MTF operating on the node to give the complete MTF acting on the node. Table 8.4 gives the resulting MTF given by either I or R operating on one of these classes. The total sign transfer function acting on the node can be built up in a similar manner. Here there are only the four possibilities $+,-,$ABS,$-$ABS.

	S	F	IM	RM	RS	IF	RIF
I	S	IF	IM	IM	S	IF	IF
R	RS	F	RM	RM	RS	RIF	RIF

Table 8.4

The type of code required where one subtree is a variable and the other the accumulator can be obtained, as before, by looking up the relevant entry in a four by four sign table and a seven by seven mode transfer table. Really, a separate four by four table is required for each entry in the seven by seven table. However, the number of different possibilities usually turns out to be quite small. Table 8.5 shows the code required for the case (ACC,V) where the sign function on both nodes is $+$. The code produced would be an ADD instruction. Table 8.5 defines whether this operation should be normalised or unnormalised and the resulting MTF still to be applied to the accumulator ACC which replaces the mode in the tree. The aim has

79

VARIABLE							
+	S	F	IM	RM	RS	IF	RIF
S	U S	N F	U S	U RS	U RS	U S	U RS
F	N F	N F	N F	N F	N F	*	*
IM	U S	N F	N IM	N RM	U RS	*	*
RM	U RS	N F	N RM	N RM	U RS	*	*
RS	U RS	N F	U RS	U RS	U RS	U RS	U RS
IF	U S	α	α	α	U RS	α	α
RIF	U RS	α	α	α	U RS	α	α

(The row labels S, F, IM, RM, RS, IF, RIF are grouped under *ACC*.)

Table 8.5

been to keep REAL quantities that are integer in value in an un-normalised form as this is the most useful of the two forms. The entries marked with * are almost certainly non-terminal positions. The accumulator will have to be stored; the integral part of the variable has to be found followed by the addition of the temporary storage containing the original value of the accumulator. When deciding which of the two sub-trees to code first, the R.T sub-tree would therefore have been computed first in this case if the L.T sub-tree was terminal. The entries marked α are probably able to take the integral part of the accumulator in the hypothetical order code without requiring any temporary storage. The unnormalised zero given earlier could be added, for example. This may not be the case for some order codes, and then these entries would also denote non-terminal positions requiring storage of the accumulator.

Most of the handling of mode transfer functions could have been used in the simple stack algorithm described initially. However, this would not normally be done, as the quality of code produced would not warrant it. The handling of mode transfer functions in the tree becomes more important as soon as the algorithm is extended to handle common sub-expressions. A single sub-tree may be pointed at from several places each with different mode transfer functions acting on the common sub-expression represented by the sub-tree. The common sub-expression would be coded and stored in a temporary storage location. The parts of the mode transfer functions not coded would then be left as unary operators between the nodes pointing at the common sub-expression and the temporary storage location.

Consider for example the Fortran expression:

ABSF(FLOATF(−XFIXF(XABSF(J))))*
XFIXF(−ABSF(FLOATF(−I*J)))

which after I*J has been coded would leave a tree as shown in Fig. 8.4 with the MTF and STF acting on the accumulator and variable J given in brackets. Calculating the total MTF and STF for the terminals gives:

MTF for *ACC* is IM
MTF for *J* is RS
STF for *ACC* is $-ABS$
STF for *J* is *ABS*

Looking up the relevant code in the seven by seven table for the multiply operator and the four by four sign table would probably define the code required as

MPYN *J*

with a MTF of RM and STF of $-ABS$ still to be applied to the terminal *ACC* which replaces this sub-tree.

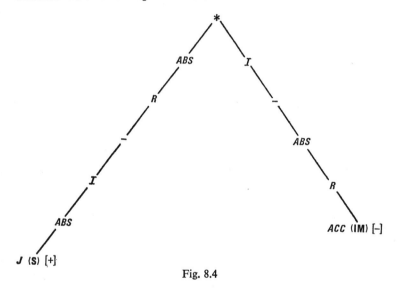

Fig. 8.4

8.7 Coding simple common sub-expressions

A *simple* common sub-expression is defined as one in which two or more appearances of the sub-expression are unaffected by any intermediate assignments. For example the arithmetic expression:

$$a + b*c + (c*b + a)*f$$

has the simple common sub-expressions $b*c$ and $a + b*c$. If the C-structure is a tree, then recognition of identical sub-trees is equivalent to finding simple common sub-expressions. There are two basically different approaches to how this should be done. The first examines the completed C-structure and by a comparison of all nodes will eventually find the common sub-expressions. This is the method used if the C-structure consists of triples as in Sheridan's algorithm. It tends to be slow as a large amount of sorting and examination is required. The second method endeavours to find the common sub-expressions as the C-structure is being generated. This is the method usually adopted with the tree algorithm and the techniques used in an implementation will be described.

It is now necessary to consider more closely how the tree is stored. As the tree node is completely defined by its two operands and operator, these can be used as a key to look up the node in what is known as a *graph table*. If the node already appears in the table, then a similar node has appeared before and this must therefore be a common sub-expression. Instead of producing another identical entry, the same entry is used for both occurrences of the common sub-expression. The tree has now become a directed graph as two pointers exist to a node. The graph for $a + b*c + (c*b + a)*f$ is given in Fig. 8.5. The most likely type of table to use for storing the

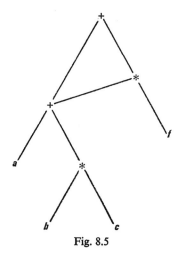

Fig. 8.5

graph would be a hash table. The use of the stack for the expression above is shown in Fig. 8.6. Table 8.6 shows the graph table as a simple look up table. As each operand is to be loaded into the stack, it is first looked-up in the graph table and, if present, this entry position is loaded into the stack. If not, then a new entry is formed in the graph table. This is made to look like a normal node by having a null left operand and a zero operator. The fourth column shown in the graph table contains the *occurrence number* which contains the number of times that a pointer to the node has appeared in the graph. It is set to one when the entry is first defined and is only defined for non-terminals.

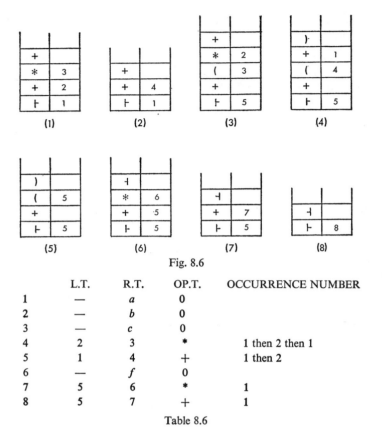

Fig. 8.6

	L.T.	R.T.	OP.T.	OCCURRENCE NUMBER
1	—	a	0	
2	—	b	0	
3	—	c	0	
4	2	3	*	1 then 2 then 1
5	1	4	+	1 then 2
6	—	f	0	
7	5	6	*	1
8	5	7	+	1

Table 8.6

In the example, the stack is filled initially until combination occurs for the operator * causing the entry 4 in the graph table. If the operator is commutative, then the operands are entered in the dictionary with L.T having the lower position in the graph table. At stage (3), combination occurs for the node defined by 3*2 (L.T is the entry 3 in the graph table; entry 2 is R.T; the operator is *). This is rearranged at 2*3 (* is commutative) and, on look-up, this entry is found to be already in the table at position 4. This is a common sub-expression and the occurrence number is incremented (now set to 2). At stage (4) in the stacking, the node 4 + 1 is equivalent to 1 + 4 (+ is commutative) and this already appears in the graph table as entry 5. The occurrence number of entry 5 is therefore incremented to give the value 2. At this stage the sub-expression $a + b*c$ has been recognised as common and also the expression $b*c$. As $b*c$ is part of the larger common sub-expression and as it will not be pointed at directly a second time, the occurrence number for entry 4 is decreased by 1 leaving it with the value 1. Explicitly, the action taken when a node is found to be already in the table is as follows:

The occurrence number for the node is incremented by 1 and, if the occurrence number of L.T is greater than 1 then it is decreased by 1, and similarly for R.T.

The algorithm for code generation will now of course have to be modified to take account of common sub-expressions. The function $C(T)$ is the same except that, after generating the code for node T, the occurrence number of T is examined and, if greater than 1, the code

ST *TEMP*

is generated and the tree node changed to the terminal *TEMP*. Later in the code generation, when alternative paths of the graph arrive at this point, the value of the common sub-expression that is stored in *TEMP* will be used instead of coding it again. The reason for decreasing the occurrence number of $b*c$ is now obvious, as otherwise an unnecessary ST instruction would have been generated.

The presence of common sub-expressions also influences the choice of paths through the graph when generating code. As shown before, there is a certain amount of flexibility allowed in which sub-tree to code first when both L.T and R.T are nonterminal. However, if one of the sub-trees is a common sub-expression then this needs to be stored in any case so that *this* would seem to be the sub-tree to code first. For example, $E + b*c$ where E represents a common sub-expression would best be coded as:

```
C(E)
ST     TEMP
L      b
MPY    c
ADD    TEMP
```

The value of *TEMP* would then be used whenever code was wanted for the second and subsequent appearances of the common sub-expression. However, this is not completely correct as another use of E might appear in the coding of the other sub-tree. Consider for example $(a + E)*E$. When coding the node T, where OP.T = * and L.T is the expression $a + E$ and R.T = E, it would be wrong to code the right sub-tree first as this would produce the following code:

```
C(E)
ST     TEMP
L      a
ADD    TEMP
MPY    TEMP
```

A load operation can be avoided by coding the left sub-tree

$$C(E)$$
ST   *TEMP*
ADD   *a*
MPY   *TEMP*

The general rule is, therefore: if R.T is a common sub-expression and the same common sub-expression appears as part of L.T, then code L.T first, otherwise code R.T first (similarly for R.T being a common sub-expression). It is usually impracticable to do a deep search for the common sub-expression but it might be worth going down a depth of one or two levels in the graph.

8.8 Coding sets of assignment statements

The benefits gained from coding several statements together, rather than separately, are mainly that common sub-expressions can be found over a larger distance and the reloading of values after assignment (if required in the next statement) can be avoided. It may be possible to permute the order of execution of statements to produce better code, although care must obviously be taken that the assigned values are not used in the statements between those permuted.

Sets of assignment statements will be considered which have no path of control into the set other than at the top and which exit at the bottom. The only addition to the tree algorithm, defined so far, is to have a means of linking the separate trees of the individual statements together. An obvious method is to have a *statement list* which points to the = nodes of the statements as they appear. For example the statements

$$a = b*c + d$$
$$e = b*c + f$$

would produce a graph as shown in Fig. 8.7. The circled numbers denote the position of the statement in the statement list.

8.8.1 *Bogus common sub-expressions*

Once assignments to variables can occur, it is possible to pick up bogus common sub-expressions unless care is taken. For example:

$$a = b*c$$
$$c = d$$
$$e = c*b$$

The expression $b*c$ is not common, as an assignment to the variable c occurs in an intervening statement. Probably the simplest method of avoiding this recognition is to *substitute* the right hand side of an

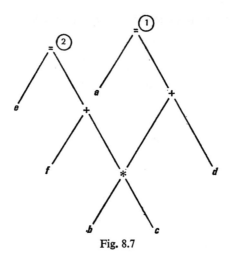

Fig. 8.7

assignment statement for the left hand variable whenever the left hand variable appears in future statements. This will require an extra entry in the graph table pointing back from the assigned variable to the = node. This will be called the *LHS back link* (Left Hand Side). The rule adopted is as follows:

Before using any graph table entry to produce a new node, it is first examined to see if the LHS back link is set and, if so, the entry pointed to by the LHS back link is used instead. The example above would produce the tree shown in Fig. 8.8.

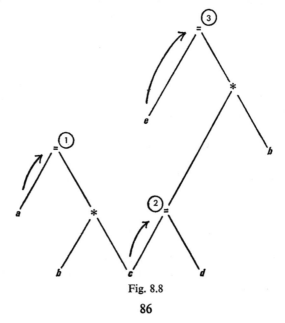

Fig. 8.8

8.8.2 *Statement rearrangement*

Consider the example:

$$a = b*c$$
$$d = e$$
$$f = a + b$$

If taken in order, code produced for these statements would be:

L	b	instead of the optimal code	L	e
MPY	c		ST	d
ST	a		L	b
L	e		MPY	c
ST	d		ST	a
L	a		ADD	b
ADD	b		ST	f
ST	f			

It is necessary to delay the coding of the first statement if it is substituted in a later statement. However, there are dangers in such an action. Consider for example:

$$a = b*c$$
$$c = e$$
$$f = a + c$$

where it would be wrong to make any rearrangement in the order. A simple rule to decide whether or not to delay the coding of a statement is as follows:

If a statement V assigns a value to the variable b and a later statement X uses b on the right hand side, then the coding of V can be delayed and included in the coding of X only if none of the intervening statements change any of the variables used on the right hand side of statement V.

This can be implemented by having two additional columns in the graph table for the following entities:

(1) Coupling Bit. This is set *on* for an = node as soon as the assignment is made and when *on* implies that there is no reason why this statement has to be coded at this point. The bit is set *off* as soon as any of the variables on the right hand side of this assignment statement are changed by subsequent assignment statements.

(2) Delay Bit. If a statement V assigns a value to the variable b and later b is used in another statement then, when this substitution takes place, if the coupling bit for the = node of V is still *on*, then the delay bit is set. Code is then produced by taking each statement in turn from the statement list and coding it unless the delay bit is set. No code is produced for the statement in its correct position if the

delay bit is set. Instead code will be generated at the same time as the statement that it has been substituted in.

Consider how these bits would be used in the following example:

$$a = b*c$$
$$c = d + g$$
$$e = b*c$$
$$f = a$$

At each production of an $=$ node in the graph, the coupling bit must be set for that statement, and the coupling bits must be set *off* for all statements that used the assigned variable previous to this. The LHS back link must also be set pointing back to the $=$ node. At each substitution the delay bit is set if possible. The graph table with the additional columns, LHS back link (*LHS*), coupling bit (*CB*) and delay bit (*DB*), is shown for the completed graph in Table 8.7 and the graph itself is given in Fig. 8.9. The coupling bit for the first statement (entry 5) is put *on* initially but is turned *off* by the following

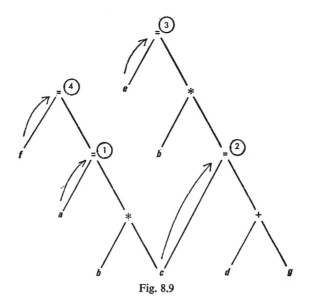

Fig. 8.9

assignment statement (entry 9). However, when the substitution for the variable '*c*' occurs in the third statement, the coupling bit for the second statement will still be *on* so that the delay bit will be set for the second statement. The substitution for the variable '*a*' in the fourth statement will not cause the delay bit of the first statement to be set as the coupling bit has already been turned *off*.

	L.T.	R.T.	OP.T	*LHS*	*DB*	*CB*
1	—	a	o	5	o	
2	—	b	o			
3	—	c	o	9		
4	2	3	*			
5	1	4	=		o	1 then o
6	—	d	o			
7	—	g	o			
8	6	7	+			
9	3	8	=		1	1
10	—	e	o	12		
11	2	9	*			
12	10	11	=			1
13	—	f	o	14		
14	13	5	=			1

Table 8.7

Code is generated for statements 1, 3 and 4 in that order. The second statement will be coded as part of the third as the delay bit is *on*. The code produced would therefore be:

```
L     b
MPY   c
ST    a
L     d
ADD   g
ST    c
MPY   b
ST    e
L     a
ST    f
```

At an assignment, the coupling bits for all statements using the assigned variable on the right hand side must be set *off*. This can be arranged by having a unique position in a bit vector assigned to each variable as it appears in the sequence of statements. With each tree node can be associated a bit vector with bits set in the positions corresponding to the variables which appear as operands in the complete sub-tree of this node. With each = node is, therefore, a bit vector which defines which variables appear on the right hand side. These can be interrogated at an assignment to see if the assigned variable has been used in any of the statements preceding it in the statement list. To avoid requiring a vector of unknown length, a set length can be defined and the last bit can be used to refer to the whole class of subsequent variables which are used after the other bits of the vector have been allocated. This obviously may cause more inefficient code to be produced, but it could be used as a rescue procedure until the end of the current assignment statement. Instead of producing the C-structure for the next statement, those statements already analysed would be coded.

A set of statements coded together in this way must, of course, have no paths of control arriving at an intermediate point in the sequence as well as at the top. Consequently a labelled statement would cause the termination of the preceding sequence and the start of another, unless information is known about this alternative entry. Sometimes this information is available in the language definition. For example, the control variable in a Fortran DO statement cannot be altered in the body of the DO statement so that, even if several paths exist through the DO, these are known not to alter the controlled variable and, as far as it is concerned, the whole DO statement could be treated as a single sequence.

8.9 Global optimisation

So far, the algorithms described have been dealing with sets of arithmetic statements with the only path of control entering at the top and leaving at the bottom. The next sophistication would be to attempt to produce code for larger pieces of program with a control structure which could be represented by a directed graph and with assignment statements and expressions to be evaluated on the paths joining the nodes. The emphasis is now not so much on finding common sub-expressions but on moving the evaluation of expressions or assignments from one part of a program to a more advantageous one. The simplest example is an expression evaluated within a loop whose components are not assigned inside the loop. It would clearly have been better to have calculated the expression just once outside the loop.

Another example is the case where several branches meet at a point in the program and all but one require an expression to be evaluated. This same expression is required after the conjunction. In this case it would be better to force the evaluation of the expression in the branch where it was not required and remove it from the position after the join. The expression can then be assumed to be available from *all* branches at the conjunction, and it will not be necessary to recalculate the common sub-expression.

Several attempts to produce general algorithms of this form have been made. None has been completely successful as yet. All tend to be time consuming as the process has to be done recursively on simple graphical forms, and it is not obvious how much more efficient the final code produced by such an algorithm will be. Also the user tends not to be too happy with a code generator which reorders his code to such an extent that it is often quite difficult to find out where a program has reached in execution.

9

STORAGE ALLOCATION

9.1 Introduction

The allocation of storage for 'programmer defined' variables in a higher level language is usually straightforward. The languages in use today have been designed so that storage allocation is to a large extent under the control of the user. Consequently, efficient utilisation of storage is the programmer's problem and not the compiler writer's. In Fortran, for example, there are basically only two types of variables. The COMMON variables are global to all routines and must be allocated a length of storage specified by the user. The user defines how this storage is structured, and there is little to be done by the compiler. The LOCAL variables give a little more scope in deciding how storage should be allocated for them. Unless an EQUIVALENCE declaration has been used, there is no assumed relationship between these variables, and storage can be allocated in an order and position that is defined by the compiler. Usually the only important decision is where these variables are stored. Allocation is often done in an area of storage immediately following the routine in question. However, with modern computers and operating systems requiring fixed and variable parts of a program to be separated, allocation in a separate area is becoming more necessary.

In Algol, recursion makes storage allocation slightly more difficult. As each variable defined in a recursive procedure must have storage allocated for it at each level of recursion, it is necessary to define a stack in which storage is allocated to variables as each block is entered and storage is released as each block is left. A good description of such a system is given by Irons and Feurzeig (1961).

The major problems of storage allocation arise when considering how to allocate storage for temporary variables required for partial results during a compilation. These variables are not defined by the language but by the compiler. How many are required and how storage is allocated is completely dependent upon the compiler. Consequently an algorithm is required which will make the allocation most efficient. Efficiency in this context will usually mean attempting to minimise the amount of storage used.

Storage allocation also becomes a problem as soon as the computer does not have a single-level of storage. Problems concerning efficient usage of main and backing storage are out of the scope of this book and are usually dealt with by operating systems surrounding a compiler. However, many computers have a limited set of *fast registers* with either a much quicker access time than main storage or alternatively more desirable properties. Using such registers efficiently is up to the compiler and algorithms must be defined which allocate these fast registers to variables in the most advantageous way. Many computers have a set of index registers which fall into this category of fast registers. Similarly a multi-accumulator computer would be considered as having the additional accumulators as fast registers.

9.2 Allocating storage for temporary variables

The algorithm to be discussed here is basically for allocating storage to temporary variables required for short periods during a calculation. In Chapter 8 it was necessary to use temporary working spaces for storing parts of an expression that had already been calculated while another part was being calculated. The code generation algorithms did not concern themselves with how storage, for these temporary variables, should be allocated. They can be thought of as taking a new variable name from an infinite set of unused names each time a temporary variable is required by the algorithm. The storage allocation algorithm has to allocate storage for these variables in such a way that the minimum number of storage locations is required. Obviously, variables having completely disjoint ranges can be allocated the same storage. The *range* of a variable is defined as the time interval between the initial definition of a variable and its last use.

Consider a set of variables V_1, V_2, V_3, ..., V_n. For each variable V_i, an instruction is defined:

$$\text{ST} \quad V_i$$

which initially sets a value to the variable and indicates the start of the range for V_i. An instruction:

$$\text{U} \quad V_i$$

is defined which indicates a subsequent use of this variable. The last instruction of this type using V_i indicates the end of the range for V_i. This instruction will be used to represent instructions such as ADD, SUB etc. defined in Chapter 8.

A sequence of code produced by the code generator then consists of a set of instructions independent of the V_i together with orders of the two types defined above which use the variables V_i for $i = 1$ to n. The problem is to allocate storage to the V_i so that the minimum number of locations is required. The assumption is that a variable is no longer required after the last appearance of it in the sequence.

In this sense it is assumed that the sequence is complete. Once a variable is no longer required, its storage location may be re-allocated to another variable not yet defined. It is assumed that this sequence of instructions does not contain any entry points other than at the top and that control passes straight through the sequence leaving at the bottom.

For example the tree algorithm in Chapter 8 would produce code for the expression given in Table 8.2 as follows:

$$
\begin{array}{ll}
\text{L} & h \\
\text{ADD} & k \\
\text{ST} & V_1 \\
\text{L} & d \\
\text{ADD} & e \\
\text{DIV} & V_1 \\
\text{ST} & V_2 \\
\text{L} & f \\
\text{MPY} & g \\
\text{SUB} & V_2 \\
\text{ST} & V_3 \\
\text{L} & b \\
\text{MPY} & c \\
\text{ADD} & a \\
\text{DIV} & V_3
\end{array}
$$

The names V_1, V_2 and V_3 would be taken from the set of unused names. The storage allocation algorithm to be defined would show that in fact these three variables can all use the same storage location T_1. As far as the storage allocation algorithm is concerned the significant parts of the sequence can be written:

$$
\begin{array}{ll}
\text{ST} & V_1 \\
\text{U} & V_1 \\
\text{ST} & V_2 \\
\text{U} & V_2 \\
\text{ST} & V_3 \\
\text{U} & V_3
\end{array}
$$

As the last use of each variable appears before the next is defined, it is easily seen that one storage location is sufficient.

Suppose that a stack of unused storage locations written $[T_1, T_2, T_3, \ldots]$ is available, and suppose that each time a location is required one is taken from the top of the stack and that these locations are returned to the stack as soon as the last use of the variable to which it is allocated appears. The simplest description of the algorithm is then as follows:

Scan the sequence of instructions *from the end backwards*. For each instruction of the type U V_i if no storage location has been allocated to V_i, take the top free storage location from the stack and assign it to V_i and replace V_i in the instruction by the address of the storage location. This replacement is also done in the case where the storage allocation had been done previously. For each instruction ST V_i, if no storage location has been allocated to V_i then either there is an error or this order is redundant as this implies that there are no subsequent uses of the variable. If storage has been allocated to V_i then replace V_i in the instruction by the address of the storage location and, as this is the first use of the variable V_i, the location may now be returned to the free store stack as it is no longer required. Dantzig and Reynolds (1966) have shown that this algorithm is optimal although not uniquely so.

Consider for example:

(1) ST V_1
(2) ST V_2
(3) U V_2
(4) U V_1
(5) ST V_3
(6) U V_1
(7) U V_3
(8) ST V_4
(9) U V_3
(10) U V_4

and assume the free storage stack is $[T_1, T_2, T_3]$. Scanning from the end, (10) will cause V_4 to be allocated storage T_1 and (9) will allocate T_2 to V_3 leaving the stack as $[T_3]$. Instruction (8) will release T_1 so that the stack is then $[T_1, T_3]$ and (6) will cause V_1 to be allocated to T_1. Similarly (5) releases T_2 which is then allocated to V_2 by instruction (3). The code produced is therefore:

(1) ST T_1
(2) ST T_2
(3) U T_2
(4) U T_1
(5) ST T_2
(6) U T_1
(7) U T_2
(8) ST T_1
(9) U T_2
(10) U T_1

The algorithm finds the range of each variable by using the first appearance of the variable in the backward scan to define the end of the range and the corresponding ST instruction to define the start of the range. This is all that is required, and the algorithm can be modified to use a forward scan to produce this information. In the forward scan, the ST instruction defines the start of the range as before. If a count of the number of uses of each variable has been kept then the last use of a variable can also be found, so that the end of the range is known. In the tree algorithm defined in Section 8.7, the occurrence number contains a count of the number of uses of a variable and could therefore be used for this purpose.

Another alternative is to locate the end of the range by the method described in the backward technique although in fact scanning forwards. This is achieved by chaining together all the uses of a particular variable as they are scanned. Associated with each variable V_i are three locations F_i, L_i and R_i. F_i is the position of the ST instruction for V_i and L_i is the position of the last use of V_i. The range of V_i is therefore (F_i, L_i). R_i contains the location assigned to V_i and this is set initially to zero.

As the sequence of instructions is scanned, a ST V_i instruction will cause F_i and L_i to be set to contain the position of this instruction in the sequence. An instruction U V_i will cause the contents of L_i to be set in place of V_i in this instruction and L_i changed to contain the position of this instruction. In the example above the final values of F_i and L_i are as follows:

$$F_1 = 1 \qquad L_1 = 6$$
$$F_2 = 2 \qquad L_2 = 3$$
$$F_3 = 5 \qquad L_3 = 9$$
$$F_4 = 8 \qquad L_4 = 10$$

and the instructions will be:

    (1) ST 0
    (2) ST 0
    (3) U   2
    (4) U   1
    (5) ST 0
    (6) U   4
    (7) U   5
    (8) ST 0
    (9) U   7
    (10) U   8

At the end of the scan, L_i points to a chain through the uses of the variable V_i. Each instruction contains the position of the next instruction in the chain in the address part. Once a location has been assigned to V_i, then it is a simple matter to move down the chain replacing the address parts of the instruction by the location assigned to V_i. The range for each variable is now defined by the pair (F_i, L_i). These pairs can now be scanned to allocate storage to each variable. If $F_i = L_i$ then the ST instruction is redundant as before.

The ranges are scanned in ascending order of F_i and, in the example, the variables are already defined in this order. Usually the code generation algorithm can be linked to the storage allocation algorithm so that this is always the case. It just requires that the order in which variable names appear for the first time in the sequence of instructions is the same order as positions given in the vectors for F_i and L_i. In the example V_1 must be defined before V_2 and so on.

Scanning in ascending order of F_i, the first variable is allocated T_1. For each subsequent range (F_j, L_j), the *active* ranges, already with storage allocated, are examined to see if a range exists, call it (F_i, L_i), such that $L_i < F_j$. If a range exists, then V_j is allocated the same storage location as V_i and the range (F_i, L_i) is marked as *inactive*. At each stage therefore the active ranges define the current variables to which the locations are allocated, and when these locations will become free. If no range exists with $L_i < F_j$, a new location must be taken from the stack and allocated to V_j.

In the example, V_1 would be allocated T_1. As $L_1 > F_2$, a new location is required for V_2 and so this would be allocated T_2. However, $L_2 < F_3$ so V_3 can use the same location as V_2 (that is T_2). The range for V_2 is now marked as inactive. As $L_1 < F_4$, V_4 is also allocated T_1.

9.3 The Belady algorithm

Some computers have a small number of fast registers which are similar to main storage except that the time required to access information stored in the fast registers is very much less than the access time for main storage. They may, in fact, be index registers or additional accumulators which can use their contents in arithmetic or logical operations, but such properties will be ignored at present.

These fast registers can be used to contain copies of variables which have been allocated main storage and, in the case of a temporary variable, it may be that it can reside in a fast register for its entire existence so that no main storage need be allocated. As long as there are more fast registers available than variables required, there is no problem and the fast registers can be allocated by an algorithm like those described in Section 9.2. The situation will, however, arise when the number of fast registers available is inadequate, and a decision has to be made as to which of the variables should continue to reside in the fast registers. This will depend on the frequency of use of the different variables and the algorithm must aim to maximise the utilisation of the fast registers.

The Belady algorithm is one which produces an optimal result for a rather restricted situation and often gives good results in more general cases. It is assumed that the fast registers are to be used to contain copies of the variables in main storage and that it is only possible to operate on these variables by first loading them into fast registers. An example of a computer of this type is the CDC 6600. At the moment it will be assumed that these variables will not be altered, so that if a variable in a fast register is to be replaced, it is not necessary to store the current contents of the fast register as a copy exists in main storage already.

The problem is analogous to the replacement of pages in a two-level storage system. For example, on a computer with main storage and a drum for backing storage, it is often necessary to keep parts of a program and its data in the main store and the remainder on the drum. The program and its data can only be accessed from the main store but not from the drum. When a part of the program is required which is currently on the drum, it is necessary to remove a section or page from the main store and replace it by the relevant page of drum storage. Various algorithms are used to decide which page of main store to remove but all tend to be inefficient as future accesses to the various pages in main store is unknown when the decision has to be made. An optimal algorithm was defined by Belady (1966) in the case where the complete pattern of future accesses is known. This has been used in the two-level storage system to give a measure of the efficiency of the many heuristics adopted. The allocation of fast registers differs from the two-level storage problem as allocation need not be done until a complete sequence of code is available. Consequently, the Belady algorithm itself can be used to give optimal results. The algorithm has been used for several years in compilers and it is only recently through its use in the two-level storage system that the name Belady has been associated with it.

The ranges in which the main variables V_i are used can be shown by a diagram like Fig. 9.1. Each horizontal line represents the range of a variable with the dots giving positions in the instruction sequence where the variable is used. It will be assumed that only one variable is used in each instruction so that two or more dots cannot appear on a vertical line. The left hand end defines the instruction where the

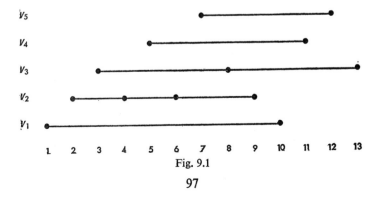

Fig. 9.1

97

variable was first used and the right hand end defines the last use. The number of lines intersected by a vertical line indicates the number of storage locations that are in use at that point. If a vertical line intersects more lines than the number of fast registers available then one or more of the variables cannot reside in the fast registers.

Each time a variable is accessed from a fast register it will be assumed that this takes a negligible amount of time. If a variable is not available in a fast register then the contents of one of the fast registers must be replaced by the required variable. If a function $S(i,t)$ is defined where:

$S(i,t) = 0$ if V_i is not in a fast register at time t.
$S(i,t) = 1$ if V_i is available in a fast register at time t.

then for each point 't' in the sequence:

$$\sum S(i,t) \leq N$$

where N is the number of fast registers available (N is assumed independent of t). If $m(t)$ is defined as the number of the variable used in instruction 't' then a utilisation function U can be defined as:

$$U = \sum_t S(m(t),t)$$

The maximum value of U (subject to the constraints given above) will ensure that most uses of variables will take place from the fast registers. The only other constraint is that:

$$S(m(t-1),t) = 1$$

for all t. This ensures that each variable is brought to a fast register when used. The Belady algorithm for producing an optimal solution to the problem is as follows:

The sequence is examined starting at the first instruction defined at $t = 1$ in Fig. 9.1. For each t the variable V_i where $i = m(t)$ is examined and action taken as follows:

(1) The variable V_i has a fast register allocated to it and therefore this register is used.

(2) No fast register is allocated to V_i but an unused fast register is available and so this is allocated to V_i.

(3) The variable V_i has no fast register allocated to it and *all* fast registers are allocated. The variables currently having a copy in the fast registers are examined and if one is no longer required then this fast register is reallocated to V_i. If all fast registers are still in use then *the variable whose next use is furthest away from this point has its fast register reallocated to V_i*.

In the example given in Fig. 9.1, consider the case where three fast registers are available and call them R_1, R_2 and R_3. Starting from

$t = 1$ the first three instructions will cause R_1, R_2 and R_3 to be allocated to V_1, V_2 and V_3. At $t = 5$ all three fast registers are still in use but a register is required for V_4. V_1 is not used again until $t = 10$ whereas V_2 is used at $t = 6$ and V_3 at $t = 8$. Therefore R_1 is reallocated to V_4. At $t = 7$ the problem arises again. V_4 is not required until $t = 11$ whereas V_3 is used at $t = 8$ and V_2 at $t = 9$. Therefore R_1 is now reallocated to V_5. At $t = 10$, V_1 is used once more. Condition (2) above now applies as V_2 is no longer required. R_2 is therefore allocated to V_1. Similarly, at $t = 11$ R_2 is reallocated to V_4 as V_1 is now no longer required. R_1 and R_3 continue to be allocated to V_5 and V_3 until the end of the sequence. This allocation of fast registers is shown diagrammatically in Fig. 9.2.

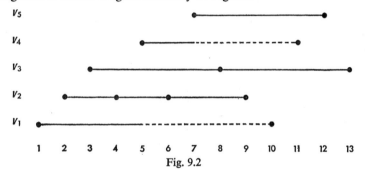

Fig. 9.2

9.4 Index register allocation

The Belady algorithm is only optimal for a very limited set of problems although it is usually an effective algorithm in many other cases. This is intuitively reasonable, for each time a register has to be re-allocated, the aim is to remove the variable which will keep the problem from reappearing for the longest possible time. The Belady algorithm is not optimal as soon as the cost for removing each variable is different.

The example given in Section 9.3 of a set of fast registers being allocated to variables in main store could be extended so that these variables can be altered as well as used. A sequence of variables used will be written:

$$(V_i, V_j, V_k, V_l, \ldots)$$

This notation implies that variable V_i is used, followed by the use of variable V_j and so on. The example in Fig. 9.1 can then be written as $(V_1, V_2, V_3, V_2, V_4, V_2, V_5, V_3, V_2, V_1, V_4, V_5, V_3)$. A variable which is altered as well as used will be denoted by * following the name of the variable. For example (V_1, V_2^*, V_1) will denote a sequence of instructions which uses V_1, uses and resets V_2, then uses V_1 again. If the copy of a variable that has been loaded into an index register is altered and later the register is re-allocated to another variable, then the contents of the index register must overwrite the old value of the variable in main store and the new variable loaded into the index register. This requires two store accesses and so the cost of such an operation should be 2 units compared with 1 when the old variable has not been altered.

Consider, for example, a sequence (V_1, V_2, V_3^*, V_2) and two index registers containing initially V_2 and V_3^*. The Belady algorithm would cause the contents of the index registers to be altered as follows:

Sequence	Index Registers	Cost
	$V_2 V_3^*$	
V_1	$V_2 V_1$	2
V_2	$V_2 V_1$	0
V_3^*	$V_2 V_3^*$	1
V_2	$V_2 V_3^*$	0

however:

Sequence	Index Registers	Cost
	$V_2 V_3^*$	
V_1	$V_1 V_3^*$	1
V_2	$V_2 V_3^*$	1
V_3^*	$V_2 V_3^*$	0
V_2	$V_2 V_3^*$	0

This has a total cost of 2 units. The Belady algorithm breaks down because of the 2 unit cost of removing V_3 when it is going to be modified later on, so that this modified value in main store is never used.

Starting at the head of the sequence, there is an initial configuration of the index registers and a finite number of changes which can be made to their contents so that the variable required in the first position of the sequence is available in an index register. Each of the configurations arrived at after the first variable in the sequence has been allocated an index register is now examined in turn. Each of these generates a finite set of configurations which load the second variable into an index register and so on. A complete graph can be built up of all the possible different states that the index registers may pass through as the sequence is evaluated. This is shown in Fig. 9.3 for the example above. Associated with each transition from one state to another is a certain cost and this is marked on the line joining the two states. With each state is marked in brackets the minimum cost required to arrive at this state. For a complete sequence, the path with minimum cost to the final step is the optimal one required. General algorithms for finding shortest paths have been in use for many years (see Dantzig (1960)) and algorithms of this type would solve the problem. However, the type of graph that appears in index register allocation is a subset of the general class and special algorithms can be used to prune the graph.

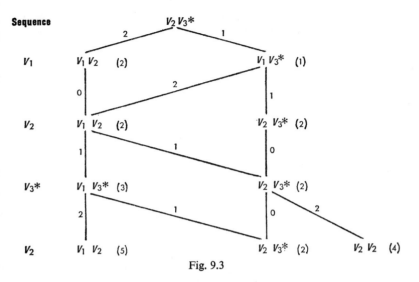

Fig. 9.3

Such an algorithm is described by Horwitz, Karp, Miller, and Winograd (1966). This paper first defines a set of possible paths from each node which are *minimal change branches*. It proves that a shortest path does exist through the graph consisting of only minimal change branches. As only one such path is required it is necessary to generate only minimal change branches.

Possible minimal change branches are defined as follows:

(1) If the variable used at the next step in the sequence is already in an index register then this is used rather than loading a second copy of the variable into another index register. If the variable is modified by the step then the variable in the final configuration will be marked with * even if the original was not.
(2) If the variable used at the next step is not in an index register, then *only one* variable is removed from an index register and replaced by the required variable. No other changes are made.

Both of these rules are intuitively reasonable, and in producing Fig. 9.3 the second had already been applied. Therefore Fig. 9.3 is strictly only a subgraph of the complete graph. Removing paths which are not minimal change branches because they violate (1) would cause the node $V_2 V_2$ to be removed from Fig. 9.3. The graph can be further pruned as it is being produced by a set of rules which can be shown to leave at least one shortest path. These rules are as follows:

(1) If several branches arrive at a node then only one branch

need be kept and this must be one of the paths which give minimum cost at this position.

(2) A node having no branches leaving it can be eliminated together with all the branches pointing at that node.

(3) If at some level it is possible to show that one of the existing nodes (call it A) can be changed into another node (call it B) on the same level (same point in the sequence of instructions) and the total cost to arrive at node B by this path is less than or equal to the minimum cost for node B then node B can be eliminated.

In the example in Fig. 9.3, on the lowest level $V_2 V_3^*$ can be changed to $V_1 V_2$ at a cost of 2 units. Arriving here by this path would therefore cost 4 whereas the minimum cost for $V_1 V_2$ is 5 units. $V_1 V_2$ can therefore be eliminated by rule (3). The path from $V_1 V_3^*$ to $V_2 V_3^*$ does not produce a minimum cost at $V_2 V_3^*$ and so this path can be eliminated by (1). $V_1 V_3^*$ now has no branches leaving it and so is removed by (2). Repetition of the use of rules (1) and (2) will eventually reduce the graph to Fig. 9.4 where only the minimum path is left.

Sequence	
	$V_2 V_3^*$
	$\Big\vert 1$
V_1	$V_1 V_3^*$ (1)
	$\Big\vert 1$
V_2	$V_2 V_3^*$ (2)
	$\Big\vert 0$
V_3^*	$V_2 V_3^*$ (2)
	$\Big\vert 0$
V_2	$V_2 V_3^*$ (2)

Fig. 9.4

In general, the rules described above will not reduce the graph to a single path and if a large number of variables and index registers is available then the size of the graph could still be too large to enumerate completely. Two additional rules which involve look ahead are therefore introduced to prune the graph still further.

The first rule is merely an extension of the rule used in the Belady algorithm. As was shown earlier, the Belady algorithm is no longer applicable and the reason is that the cost of storing an altered variable is now 2 and this makes it more desirable to keep it in the index register if possible.

(4) If a variable in an index register is no longer required then this should be replaced when an index register is required. If all variables in index registers are still required and the next step uses a variable not available in an index register then each pair

of variables V_i and V_j currently resident in index registers are considered. V_i should not be removed if:

(a) V_i and V_j are in index registers and the next appearance of either V_i or V_i^* appears before the next appearance of V_j or V_j^*.

(b) V_i^* and either V_j or V_j^* are in index registers and the next appearance of V_i^* is before the next appearance of V_j or V_j^*

(5) This rule considers two nodes on the same level which differ only in the contents of one index register, and this will be defined as V_i in one node and V_j in the other. The node involving V_j can be eliminated if:

(a) V_i is in the index register and either V_j or V_j^* is in the index register at the other node. If either V_i or V_i^* appears before V_j or V_j^* in the following sequence of instructions and the minimum cost of arriving at the node involving V_i is less than or equal to the node involving V_j then the node involving V_j can be eliminated.

(b) V_i^* is in the index register at the first node and V_j at the second. If V_i^* appears before V_j or V_j^* in the following sequence and the minimum cost of getting to the node involving V_i^* is one or more less than the minimum cost of getting to the node involving V_j then the node involving V_j can be eliminated.

(c) V_i^* is in the index register at the first node and V_j^* at the second. If V_i^* appears before V_j or V_j^* in the sequence and the minimum cost of getting to the node involving V_i^* is less than the node involving V_j^* then the node involving V_j^* can be eliminated.

These rules are usually sufficient to reduce most graphs to a size where the minimum path can be found by enumeration.

In some cases the allocation can be divided into a set of sub-problems by choosing points where the original sequence is to be broken. Each sub-sequence then has its own initial configuration of the index registers and the break-point is chosen so that the final contents of the index registers at the completion of one sub-sequence are what is required to start the next sub-sequence. For example suppose that the sequence of variables is $(\ldots\ V_1^*\ V_2^*\ V_1^*\ \ldots)$ and only two index registers are available. After the second appearance of V_1^* the contents of the index registers in the minimum cost path must be V_1^* and V_2^* by rule (4) above. Therefore the sequence could be broken at this point and the remainder of the sequence treated separately with the initial configuration having the index registers set to V_1^* and V_2^*. Details of such an algorithm are given by Luccio (1967) and Belady (1966).

10

COMPILER-COMPILERS

10.1 Introduction

Producing a compiler in an assembly language can be quite tedious and time-consuming. For example, the original Fortran I compiler for the IBM 704 took eighteen man-years to produce, and about another ten man-years of effort were needed to extend this to the Fortran II version for the IBM 709 [Backus *et al.* (1957)]. With the development and understanding of compiling techniques, the man-power required has been considerably reduced but, even now, a *reasonable* compiler for a language like Algol is unlikely to take less than four man-years to write if it is hand-coded. This amount of man-power may not be available and, even if it is, it may be uneconomic to use skilled programmers in this way. Also, if the compiler is required urgently, it may well take too long to produce. There is an optimum number of people who can work together on a project of this kind (probably about four) so that, although four people could produce the compiler in a year, it would be unlikely that eight people could produce it in six months and almost certain that sixteen people could not produce it in three months.

To try and improve the speed of production of compilers and reduce the man-power required, special purpose higher level languages called *Compiler-Compilers* (abbreviated CC) have been developed. Just as the Fortran language contains statements which most scientific users require so CC languages contain statements particularly relevant to the problem of compilation. Primitive CC languages started appearing around 1958-9 and since then a large number of languages and dialects (possibly around 75) have been developed. They range from sub-languages which aid in only one particular part of the compilation process to large systems which will generate a whole compiler once the language and target computer have been defined.

Very few direct comparisons of the efficiency of hand-coded and CC generated compilers exist [but see Brooker, Morris, and Rohl (1967)] although there has been much speculation. The object code produced by a CC generated compiler should be better than that produced by a hand-written one. Optimising code generation is, to a large extent, a formulation of special cases that can be handled either more or less efficiently on a particular computer. As it is easier to do this enumeration in a higher level language, it is also likely to be more exhaustive. The language will also tend to focus attention on the areas of interest and so avoid overlooking certain features. On the other hand, the algorithms used in the CC generated compiler tend to be more generalised than the hand-coded ones. This is to allow compilers for a large range of languages to be defined without requiring too much alteration of the underlying structure. Consequently it is usual for hand-coded compilers to be smaller and compile faster than CC generated ones. However, just as higher level languages have taken over from assembly languages for coding scientific problems so CCs will take over from assembly languages for writing compilers.

In several cases the CCs used in this Chapter have had to be simplified to avoid description of features unnecessary to the example. It is important to realise that most of these CCs provide many more facilities than the ones described so that this Chapter does not do justice to any of the more powerful CCs.

10.2 What is a compiler-compiler?

An idealised form of a CC is shown producing an Algol compiler in Fig. 10.1. The syntactic and semantic definitions of Algol are input to the CC and the output consists of an Algol compiler written in some language. This would probably be similar to machine code although it could be either an assembly or higher level language. Fig. 10.1 implies that the code produced is completely dependent on the Algol definitions so that a specialised compiler for Algol is the

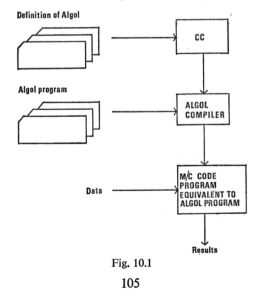

Fig. 10.1

result. Most CCs in existence tend not to approach this idealised form but more closely resemble Fig. 10.2. The CC language is often divided into a set of sub-languages each producing a specific part of the Algol compiler. For example, a special language might be defined in which to express the syntactic definition of the language; a second language might define the characteristics of the computer for which the compiler is to produce code; a third language might be used to express the semantics of the language. In many cases the output from these sub-languages are tables which drive a general purpose compiler written only once in machine code. For example, a standard top-down analysis routine might be provided in the fixed part of the compiler and this would be driven by a table produced by a special CC language in which the syntax was defined.

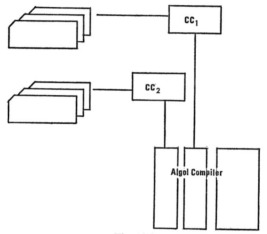

Fig. 10.2

The CC produced is, of course, capable of defining and producing the sub-compilers CC_1, CC_2, etc. Consequently it is usual, once the pilot version has been written, to produce new versions of the compilers for the sub-languages defined in terms of the complete CC. This can lead to duplication of the fixed part of the compiler unless special precautions are taken so that it is capable of driving several different sets of tables at the same time. A particular sub-class of CCs, which are easily defined in terms of themselves, is the set of CCs which are also *extendible* compilers. A good example of an extendible CC is the Brooker-Morris Compiler-Compiler (in future this will be abbreviated to BMCC. References are Brooker, Morris, and Rohl (1962) and Brooker *et al.* (1963).

The form of an extendible CC is shown in Fig. 10.3. The extendible CC (abbreviated ECC) is able to enlarge itself by defining new statements to be added to the statement repertoire of the ECC language.

106

It can, for example, add all the possible Algol statements to the existing language. The ECC language produced could then be thought of as a language with Algol as a subset. For an ECC to be a CC, it must be possible to divide the statements in the ECC language into classes so that, once the Algol statements have been defined, it is possible to state that only the class of Algol statements is expected

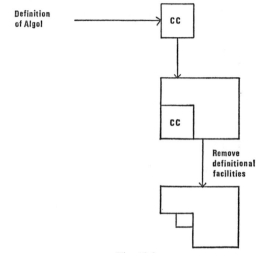

Fig. 10.3

in the program to be compiled. Once the ECC has been extended so that it can translate Algol statements as well, it is no longer necessary to keep the definitional parts of the ECC if only an Algol compiler is required. Consequently, it is usual to remove a large part of the original ECC leaving a compiler which will now only translate Algol.

10.3 Data structures

Most CCs provide the user with a certain set of data structures to aid him in the definition of the compiler. The sophistication of the CC will determine to some extent what facilities are provided. There is not, however, any direct correlation between the sophistication of the CC and the quality of the data structures provided. In the simplest kind of CC, very little is provided at all. As the CC becomes more powerful, it may provide more and more data structures together with instructions for manipulating them or alternatively it may take over complete responsibility for large sections of the compilation task but still not provide any data structures for the compiler writer. In the second case it will, of course, be using complex data structures behind the scenes but these need not become available to the user. Two examples of CCs providing data structural definitions and operations upon them are BMCC and FSL [Feldman (1964), (1966)]. The CGS system [Shapiro and Zand (1963), Zand (1964)] is an example of a sophisticated CC which does not provide data structures for the user and is arranged so that he does not need them.

BMCC basically provides the user with a list of free storage and an instruction set which maps stacks, tables, and queues on to basic list structures. Storage can be removed and returned to the free storage list. A stack (called a NEST in BMCC) can be initialised by an order:

$$B_1 = \text{NEST } (1,2,4)$$

This would set up a stack containing three levels with the constant 4 on the top level. The name of the stack is B_1. To withdraw the top element or *pop* the stack and put the contents in A_1 would require:

WITHDRAW A_1 FROM NEST B_1

while the constant 3 could be added to the stack by:

ADD 3 TO NEST B_1

Tables are arranged by having a circular list with two fields per entry; the first gives the key to the table entry while the second contains a pointer to the information part of the table entry. The entry is accessed by a statement of the form:

$$A_1 = \text{LIST } B_3 \ (\text{k, ?})$$

where B_3 is the name of the table and 'k' is the key to the table entry. The result is to put the pointer to the information part in the variable A_1.

FSL also provides tables and stacks but these are stored as vectors rather than lists. The stack orders are similar to BMCC but slightly more general. For example:

```
stack STR;
pop [STR,A₁];
push [STR,3];
STR ← 4;
```

The first line defines a stack called STR; the second removes the top element of the stack and puts it in A_1; the third adds the constant 3 to the stack. The fourth statement is not available in BMCC and overwrites the top element of the stack with the constant 4. The table orders are:

```
table SYM [200,4];
enter [SYM, FRST, 6, 8, 10 ];
A₁ ← SYM [ FRST, , $, ];
A₂ ← SYM [ 0, . , $];
```

The first defines a table of maximum length 200 with a key and 3 additional information fields; the second defines an entry in the table whose name is stored in FRST and has the information fields set to 6, 8 and 10 respectively; the third denotes a table look-up for the entry FRST which sets A_1 equal to the information field indicated by the symbol '\$', that is 8; the fourth has a zero in the key field which indicates that the same table entry is to be used as on the previous access and, in this case, the last information field is required. FSL also provides declarations for defining stacks and tables in the object program and instructions for producing code to use these in the object program.

More complex data structures can be found in languages such as BCL [Hendry (1967)], PSL, and the AED system [Ross (1967)].

10.4 Lexical analysis

The lexical analysis phase is the section of the compiler where most CCs provide little general help. The lexical analysers or *subscanners* as they are often called tend to be inflexible in the form of input they will accept. Most CCs only allow input on one peripheral device and often put restrictions on how this may be used. Consequently, it is very difficult to produce compilers with several input forms using CCs. A typical example is BMCC which has a specific subscan routine with no parameters and the only way it can be altered is for the user to replace the routine with a version of his own. This lack of a lexical scan means that it is usual for reserved words to be recognised at the syntax analysis phase. This is inefficient, and later additions to the BMCC system include a *trapdoor* from the syntax analyser back to user defined lexical analysis routines.

Most subscanners in CCs tend to use the recognition of terminal symbols as an opportunity to group these into classes so that the syntax analyser can refer to the attribute defining the class rather than the individual symbols where appropriate. For example, the declaration of terminal symbols in TGS [Dean (1964), and Plaskow and Schuman (1966)] would be:

```
BEGIN. TERMINALS
+,ADOP.
-,ADOP.
LS,RLOP.
EQ,RLOP.
BEGIN.
END. TERMINALS
```

Here + and − have been defined as belonging to the class of addition-type operators and given the attribute ADOP. Similarly, the relational operators LS and EQ have been assigned the attribute RLOP. The terminal symbol BEGIN is not assigned to any class.

In Chapter 6 a general method of lexical analysis was described using direct access tables for converting simple terminal symbols and hash tables for the reserved words. Most systems provided in CCs are not as complex as this and often simply consist of a table look-up. For example, the FSL-like CC produced at the University of Illinois [see Northcote and Steiner (1964)] has a single look-up table for storing all terminal symbols. These are precisely ordered so that the length of the reserved word can be used to point to a specific part of the table and therefore improve the length of scan required to locate a terminal symbol. The kind of directive controlling the subscanner is:

```
*PUNCS   +,-,*,/ etc.
*RESER   LS,EQ,BEGIN,PROCEDURE etc.
*EQUIV   PROCEDURE,SUBROUTINE
```

The first two statements define the terminal symbols while the third allows alternative representations of reserved words to be declared.

The subscanner is also provided with a set of small routines for analysing special input forms. For example, a routine is provided to convert all numbers appearing on the input (see Section 6.4). This is provided with parameters to allow exponents in decimal or octal, different exponentiation signs and also minor changes in the syntactic definition of a number.

10.5 Syntax analysis

It is in the area of syntax analysis that the CC has been most useful to the compiler writer. Virtually every CC provides the user with a set of statements in which to define the syntax recogniser and, in the more powerful systems, these definitions differ very little from the BNF notation often used to define the grammatical constructs in the language. Top-down analysers (see Section 7.6) and Floyd productions recognisers (see Section 7.5) are most frequently used in CCs. Precedence methods tend not to be used as the range of languages that can be handled is not large. Also, it is not easy and often impossible to generate a precedence table from a syntax defined in BNF. Consequently a CC using a precedence analyser would only be able to automate the loading of the precedence table and not the more complex problem of deciding which entries to load.

In order to give brief examples of different CCs, consider the following language defined in the notation introduced in Chapter 5:

$$P \rightarrow L .$$
$$L \rightarrow L ; S$$
$$L \rightarrow S$$
$$S \rightarrow I = E$$
$$E \rightarrow E + I$$
$$E \rightarrow I$$
$$I \rightarrow a$$
$$I \rightarrow b$$
$$I \rightarrow c$$
$$I \rightarrow d$$

The language consists of a set of assignment statements separated by ';' and terminating with '.' . Each assignment statement evaluates an expression, E, and assigns its value to one of the variables a, b, c or d. The expression consists of any set of the variables added together. An example program is:

$$a = b + c + d;$$
$$c = d + d.$$

10.5.1 *Top-down analysers*

One of the earliest CCs using a top-down analyser is the BMCC. This uses a simple non-selective top-down analyser which does not handle left recursion. Consequently the recogniser for a language like the one above, which has left recursive rules, has to be modified so that these rules do not appear. It is usual to change these to a right recursive form. The BMCC analyser for the language above could be written:

```
PHRASE [TERMINATOR] = ; , .
PHRASE [I]          = a, b, c, d
PHRASE [E]          = [I] [EXE], [I]
PHRASE [EXE]        = + [I] [EXE], + [I]
FORMAT [SS]         = [I] = [E] [TERMINATOR]
```

The PHRASE statement corresponds closely with the form of grammatical rule used in the language definition given above. Rules involving the same non-terminal on the left-hand side can be amalgamated; the different right-hand sides are separated by the symbol ';'. The non-terminal symbols are differentiated from terminal symbols by enclosing them in square brackets. The last four statements in the example language's definition therefore correspond to the second PHRASE statement given above. The left recursive definition of E has been replaced by the definitions for [E] and [EXE] in a right recursive form.

The PHRASE statement is all that is needed to define the complete syntax recogniser for the language. However, it will be necessary at some stage to take the part of the program analysed so far, find out what it means and produce code accordingly. Therefore it is necessary

111

to mark certain constructs defined by PHRASE statements so that, when this construct is recognised, a call of a semantic routine associated with this construct can be made. In BMCC a second type of PHRASE statement called the FORMAT statement is provided. The FORMAT statement resembles even more closely the language rules given in the example as only one alternative can be given per statement. With each FORMAT statement is associated a semantic routine and this is called as soon as that alternative of the non-terminal class is recognised. In the example the non-terminal class [SS] (Source Statement) has just one alternative defined which is the assignment statement. Each time an assignment statement has been analysed, the semantic routine is called and code generated before returning to analyse the next statement.

The semantic routine associated with a particular statement will, of course, require to know all the relevant information about the specific form of that statement before it can know what code to generate. In the BMCC system, the analysis routine builds up a complete parse tree (called *analysis record*) of the sentence recognised and passes this to the semantic routine. By examining this structure, the semantic routine can determine the form and meaning of the statement. The assignment statement:

$$a = b + c + d$$

would, when analysed, produce an analysis record as shown in Fig. 10.4. The tree structure produced consists of a set of nodes where each

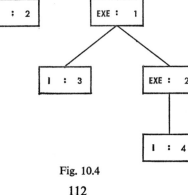

Fig. 10.4

112

node represents a non-terminal symbol that has been recognised. The number associated with each node is the alternative in the PHRASE statement that has been recognised. The nodes pointed at *from* a node denote the non-terminal symbols that appear in the alternative recognised. The terminal symbols recognised are not stored in the tree structure as these can be reconstructed from the PHRASE definitions. Apart from some redundancy that has been generated, the form of the analysis record resembles the binary tree shown in Fig. 10.5.

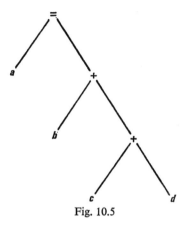

Fig. 10.5

A more powerful system than BMCC is CGS which uses a top-down analyser that *does* handle left recursion. The analyser is normally a fast-back but individual rules can be marked as slow-back where required. The notation is, of course, different but the recogniser in CGS can be written down in a form very similar to the syntactic definition of the example. The syntax of the language written in CGS is:

```
P = L $.            //              |
L = L $; S / S      //              |
S = I $= E          //GENRAT /
E = E $+ I / I      //              |
I = $a/ $b/ $c/ $d //FIXLST  /
```

In CGS terminal symbols must be preceded by the symbol $ and alternatives with the same left-hand side are separated by '/'. Instead of having a separate statement for constructs which call the semantic language, such a statement is tagged with a call such as GENRAT. Several of these calls exist but GENRAT closely resembles the call associated with a FORMAT statement in BMCC. The analyser in CGS is similar to BMCC in that it generates a tree structure to be passed to the semantic routines of the CC. However, the form of the

113

tree is considerably different, and the sub-tree produced before the call of GENRAT is shown in Fig. 10.6 for the statement:

$$a = b + c + d$$

The number associated with each node is the number of sub-trees if the node is non-terminal. Terminal elements are stored in the tree unless the particular statement is tagged with FIXLST in which case this information is not stored and the number associated with

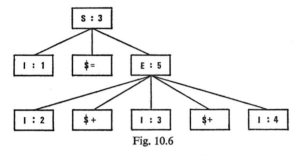

Fig. 10.6

the non-terminal node then contains the alternative recognised just as in BMCC. The other important difference is that the string of additions, instead of producing a binary tree, produce a *bushed* tree with all the identifiers involved in the additions on the same level.

10.5.2 *Floyd productions*

A good example of a CC using Floyd productions for the syntax analysis is the language FSL. The analyser is similar to the one described in Section 7.5 and shown in Table 7.3. It is less general than this as only symbols to the left of the pointer can be matched against a rule. Consequently, the pointer must first be moved over any input string of interest before checking can take place. As described in Section 7.5, the symbols to the left of the pointer are loaded into a stack so that all testing takes place on the top elements of the stack. In FSL there is a restriction that not more than the top five elements in the stack can be tested. The language has a subscan which automatically packs up identifiers so that the identifiers are converted to the class I as they are loaded into the stack. The set of productions for the example are:

LABEL	INITIAL	FINAL	NEXT	
P_1	I			$^*P_2$
P_2	I =			$^*P_3$
P_3	I = I	$\rightarrow$ I = E	$EXEC_3$	$^*E_2$
E_1	E + I	$\rightarrow$ E	$EXEC_2$	$^*E_2$
E_2	E +			$^*E_1$
	I = E ;	$\rightarrow$	$EXEC_1$	$^*P_j$
	I = E .	$\rightarrow$	$EXEC_1$	

114

Each rule consists of a label followed by the initial configuration of the stack expected for this rule to apply. This is terminated by '|' and, if an arrow follows, then the symbols in the column headed FINAL are to replace the stack elements recognised when a match occurs. The NEXT column denotes the next rule to try if this rule has been matched successfully. If this label is preceded by * then another character is read from the input into the stack before the next production is tried.

Unlike the top-down analysers described (but typical of this type of CC), no parse tree is produced automatically during the recognition process. Instead it is possible to call the semantic part of the system each time a rule is recognised. This has data structures with which the user can construct a parse tree if he desires or alternatively code may be generated each time a semantic routine is entered. In FSL the semantic routines are entered by inserting $EXEC_i$ in the production. This calls the ith semantic routine each time this production is recognised.

This type of analyser tends to be more efficient in syntax recognition than the top-down analysers although it is not as readable as the BNF-like notation used in these. However, if code is generated as syntactic productions are recognised, the code produced is not good. Recently [Earley (1965)] an algorithm has been given for converting syntax defined in BNF into an equivalent set of Floyd productions. Although the algorithm does not produce the most efficient set of Floyd productions, it could become quite important as it would allow syntax to be defined in a more readable form than Floyd productions yet still retaining the speed of syntax recognition typical of this method.

10.6 Semantic analysis

In Section 10.5 it was shown that syntax analysers tended to fall into two classes. The first calls a semantic routine each time a syntactic construct has been recognised while the second produces a parse tree for a large section of the program before passing the complete structure to a semantic routine for analysis. Most CCs using Floyd productions fall into the first class (e.g. FSL and TGS) while the top-down analysers are in both classes. Top-down analysers designed to produce efficient object code (CGS and BMCC) tend to be in the second class while simpler systems [Meta II: Schorre (1964)] are in the first class. If efficient object code is not required, the first class is usually adequate and can produce code directly (see Section 8.3). CCs in the first class which intend to produce good object code normally just pass on individual nodes of the parse tree as they are recognised, and no semantic analysis is done until the complete parse tree for a section is available. Consequently there is little difference between the methods used by semantic analysers of CCs producing good object code. Each attempts to do this by examining the form of the parse tree for a section of the program. How efficiently this can be done may well depend on the particular form of the parse tree produced. The parse tree should be kept as small as possible as this will usually save on both storage required for the tree and time required to analyse it. Usually the Floyd production recogniser is more suited to this. Not every construct recognised need add to the parse tree, and information about the parse tree can be kept in the syntactic stack until a suitable point for generation. The stack will, in any case, be used to keep pointers to the unfinished parts of the parse tree already generated. TGS is an example of a system generating a parse structure of this form. The top-down analysers tend to produce too large a parse tree unless care is taken. Syntactic classes are often defined for purely grammatical reasons causing tree nodes of little value to be introduced unless special facilities are provided to remove them. In CGS, for example, it is possible to remove some redundant nodes and also insert pointers down the most important paths through the tree.

Once the parse tree has been produced the semantic analyser must define the order in which the various parts of the tree should be examined and also recognise particular patterns in the tree which represent special cases requiring individual actions. The usual method is to enter the semantic analyser with a pointer to the top node of the tree. The form of this node and its descendants define which node or nodes should be examined next. The pointer moves about the tree in a *tree-walk* collecting information and producing code until the complete tree has been analysed,

A simplified form of the semantic analyser in CGS for the example given in Section 10.5 would be:

IF S , SON_3$ $OUTPUT(STORE,SON$_1$).
IF E , SON_1$.
IF I AND LFTSIB = $+ , $OUTPUT(ADD,SELF)
$RTSIB*RTSIB.
IF I , $OUTPUT(LOAD,SELF) $RTSIB*RTSIB.

This ordered set of rules is examined each time the pointer is moved to a new node to find the first applicable rule. This rule is then executed. The first part of the rule up to the ',' defines the type of tree node that the rule applies to. The second part of the rule defines the actions to be taken. For example, SON_1$ moves the pointer from the current node to its left most sub-node.

Consider the example given in Fig. 10.6. Initially the pointer would be set at the top node so that the first rule was applicable. The action required is first to move the pointer to the third sub-node which is the one of type E. The CGS system automatically stacks the old rule number and the position in the rule so that, when the actions for the sub-node E have been completed, the original rule can be completed. As the node is of type E, the second rule is applicable and the required action is to move the pointer to the left most sub-node of E. This is the I node representing the variable '*b*'. The third rule is not applicable as the *left sibling* (that is the node immediately to the left of the one being considered and *both* pointed at from the same node) does not exist. The fourth rule is applicable and

LOAD   *b*

is output followed by the pointer being moved to the *right sibling of the right sibling* of this node. That is the node I representing the variable '*c*'. The third rule *is* now applicable as the node to the left of this one *is* a '+' character. The operation

ADD   *c*

is output followed by moving the pointer to the last I node. This causes

ADD   *d*

to be output using the third rule. The rule now requires the pointer to move two nodes to the right again. However, no such node exists as this is the rightmost node. The system therefore assumes that the action required for this routine is complete. Retracing through the nodes, the only one not completed is the initial node S and this outputs

STORE   *a*

The BMCC tree-walk is rather different from CGS in that any number of pointers to the parse tree are allowed. This means that the control of the tree-walk cannot be defined by the position of *the* pointer as in CGS. Instead the order in which nodes are examined is controlled by a routine associated with a particular type of parse tree. Although Fig. 10.4 shows each node having its type associated with it, this is not strictly correct in BMCC. Only a number, denoting the alternative in the PHRASE statement that has been recognised, is stored in the parse tree. This is sufficient to specify the type of each node as the types can be obtained from the PHRASE statements by starting at the top of the parse tree and working downwards. In BMCC each pointer has associated with it the type of the node that it points at. A BMCC routine for analysing the parse tree for the assignment statement given as an example would be:

117

```
ROUTINE[SS] ≡ [I/1] = [E/1] [TERMINATOR/1]
              JUMP 1 IF [E/1] ≡ [I/2] [EXE/1]
              LET [E/1] ≡ [I/2]
              OUTPUT( LOAD [I/2] )
              JUMP 3
(1)           OUTPUT( LOAD [I/2] )
(2)           JUMP 4 IF [EXE/1] ≡ + [I/3] [EXE/1]
              LET [EXE/1] ≡ + [I/3]
              OUTPUT( ADD [I/3] )
(3)           OUTPUT( STORE [I/1] )
              END
(4)           OUTPUT( ADD [I/3] )
              JUMP 2
```

The variables in square brackets denote pointers to the parse tree. The first part of the name up to the symbol '/' defines the type of node pointed at while the remainder denotes which pointer variable of this type is being used. The symbol '≡' appearing in several of the statements implies that the pointer variable to the left of the symbol '≡' may be to a node whose parse tree matches that for the expression to the right of the symbol '≡'. The expression may contain pointer variables which define the type of sub-trees expected at these points. If the expression does match then these pointer variables are set to point to the corresponding sub-trees of the parse tree pointed at by the variable to the left of the symbol '≡'. For example, the initial statement of the ROUTINE given above attempts to match the parse tree with the expression:

$$[I/1] = [E/1] [TERMINATOR/1]$$

The example in Fig. 10.4 *is* an assignment statement and would therefore match this expression. Consequently the pointer variable [I/1], [E/1], and [TERMINATOR/1] would be set to point at the three sub-nodes of the node [SS]. The next statement of the routine:

$$JUMP 1 IF [E/1] ≡ [I/2] [EXE/1]$$

attempts to match the sub-tree pointed at by [E/1] with the expression [I/2] [EXE/1]. This will be successful unless the right-hand side of the assignment statement consists of a single variable. In the example, the match would be successful so [I/2] would point at the node for '*b*' and [EXE/1] set to point to the upper node of type [EXE]. As the match was successful, control is then transferred to label 1; the order:

LOAD   *b*

is output and so on. It is not necessary to restrict the matching to the nodes immediately below the node under consideration and a statement:

$$\text{JUMP 5 IF } [E/1] \equiv b + c + [I/4]$$

is allowed. The routine shown is not completely correct as it does not define the different actions required for the two possible terminators.

BIBLIOGRAPHY

This bibliography includes all the references in the text together with important papers not specifically mentioned. The following abbreviations have been used:

CACM   Communications of the Association for Computing Machinery.
JACM   Journal of the Association for Computing Machinery.
SJCC   A.F.I.P. Spring Joint Computer Conference Proceedings.
FJCC   A.F.I.P. Fall Joint Computer Conference Proceedings.

Anderson, J. P., 'A note on some compiling algorithms.' *CACM*, Vol. 7 (Mar. 1964), p. 149.

Arden, B., and Graham, R., 'On GAT and the construction of translators.' *CACM*, Vol. 2, p. 24, (July 1959).

Backus, J. W., *et al.*, 'The FORTRAN automatic coding system.' *Proceedings Western Joint C.C.*, Vol. 11, p. 188. (Feb. 1957).

Banerji, R., 'Some studies in syntax-directed parsing.' in *Computation in Linguistics*, (edit. by Garvin, P.) p. 76. (Indiana Univ. Press, 1966).

Batson, A., 'The organisation of symbol tables.' *CACM*, Vol. 8, p. 111. (Feb. 1965).

Belady, L. A., 'A study of replacement algorithms for a virtual-storage computer.' *IBM Systems Journal*, Vol. 5, No. 2, p. 78. (1966).

Brooker, R. A., Morris, D., and Rohl, J. S., 'Trees and Routines.' *Computer Journal*, Vol. 5, p. 33. (April 1962).

Brooker, R. A., *et al.*, 'The Compiler-Compiler.' *Annual Review in Automatic Programming*, Vol. 3, p. 229. (1963).

Brooker, R. A., Morris, D. and Rohl, J. S., 'Experience with the Compiler-Compiler.' *Computer Journal*, Vol. 9, p. 350. (Feb. 1967).

Brooker, R. A., 'Top-to-bottom parsing rehabilitated?' *CACM*, Vol. 10, p. 223. (April 1967).

Buchholz, W., 'File organisation and addressing.' *IBM Systems Journal*, p. 86. (June 1963).

Burkhardt, W. H., 'Universal programming languages and processors: a brief survey and new concepts.' *FJCC*, p. 1. (1965).

Cheatham, T. E., 'Theory and construction of compilers.' *Computer Associates Inc. Report*, No. CA-6606-0111. (1966).

Cheatham, T. E., and Sattley, K., 'Syntax directed compilation.' *SJCC* p. 31. (1964).

Chomsky, A. N., 'On certain formal properties of grammars.' *Information and Control*, Vol. 2, p. 137. (June 1959).

Dantzig, G. B., 'On the shortest route through a network.' *Management Science*, p. 187. (1960).

Dantzig, G. B., and Reynolds, G. H., 'Optimal assignment of computer storage by chain decomposition of partially ordered sets.' *Univ. of*

California, Berkeley *Operations Research Centre Report*, No. ORC-66-6. (March 1966).

Dean, A. L., 'Some results in the area of syntax directed compilers.' *Computer Associates Inc. Report*, No. CA-6412-0111 (Dec. 1964).

Earley, J. C., 'Generating a recogniser for a BNF grammar.' *Computation Centre Report*, Carnegie Institute of Technology. (1965).

Earley, J. C., 'An N^2 recogniser for context free grammars.' *Dept. of Computer Science Report*, Carnegie-Mellon University. (1968).

Evans, A., 'An ALGOL 60 compiler.' *Annual Review in Automatic Programming*, Vol. 4, p. 87. (1964).

Feldman, J. A., 'A formal semantics for computer-oriented languages.' *Carnegie Institute of Technology Report*. (1964).

Feldman, J. A., 'A formal semantics for computer languages and its application in a Compiler-Compiler.' *CACM*, Vol. 9, p. 3. (Jan. 1966).

Floyd, R. W., 'A descriptive language for symbol manipulation.' *JACM*, Vol. 8, p. 579. (Oct. 1961).

Floyd, R. W., 'Syntactic analysis and operator precedence.' *JACM*, Vol. 10, p. 316. (July 1963).

Floyd, R. W., 'The syntax of programming languages—a survey.' *IEEE Transactions on Electronic Computers*, EC-13, No. 4, p. 346. (Aug. 1964).

Garwick, J. V. 'GARGOYLE, a language for compiler writing.' *CACM*, Vol. 7, p. 16. (Jan. 1964.)

Ginsburg, S., 'The mathematical theory of context free languages.' *McGraw Hill.* (1966).

Glennie, A. E., 'On the syntax machine and the construction of a universal compiler.' *Carnegie Tech. Computation Centre Report*, No. 2. (July 1960).

Graham, R. M., 'Bounded context translation.' *SJCC*, p. 17. (1964).

Griffiths, T. V., and Petrick, S. R., 'On the relative efficiencies of context-free grammar recognisers.' *CACM*, Vol. 8, p. 289. (May 1965).

Hawkins, E. N., and Huxtable, D. H. R., 'A multi-pass translation scheme for Algol 60.' *Annual Review in Automatic Programming*, Vol. 3, p. 163. (1963).

Hendry, D., 'Provisional BCL Manual.' *Institute of Computer Science*, Univ. of London. (1967).

Hopgood, F. R. A., 'A solution to the table overflow problem for Hash tables.' *Computer Bulletin*, Vol. 11, p. 297. (March 1968).

Hopgood, F. R. A., and Bell, A. G., 'The Atlas Algol preprocessor for non-standard dialects.' *Computer Journal*, Vol. 9, p. 360. (Feb. 1967).

Horwitz, L. P., Karp, R. M., Miller, R. E., and Winograd, S., 'Index register allocation.' *JACM*, Vol. 13, p. 43. (Jan. 1966).

Huskey, H. D., Compiling techniques for algebraic expressions.' *Computer Journal*, Vol. 4, p. 10. (April 1961).

Iliffe, J. K., and Jodeit, J. G., 'Dynamic storage allocation.' *Computer Journal*, Vol. 5, p. 200. (Oct 1962).

Ingermann, P. Z., 'A syntax-oriented translator.' *Academic Press.* (1966).

Irons, E. T., 'A syntax-directed compiler for Algol 60.' *CACM*, Vol. 4, p. 51. (Jan. 1961).

Irons, E. T., 'The structure and use of the syntax-directed compiler.' *Annual Review in Automatic Programming*, Vol. 3, p. 207. (1963).

Irons, E. T., and Feurzeig, W., 'Comments on the implementation of recursive procedures and blocks in Algol 60.' *CACM*, Vol. 4, p. 65. (Jan. 1961).

Iverson, K. E., 'A programming language.' *John Wiley*, p. 144. (1962).

Kanner, H., Kosinski, P., and Robinson, C. L., 'The structure of yet another Algol compiler.' *CACM*, Vol. 8, p. 427. (July 1965).

Knuth, D. E., 'RUNCIBLE—algebraic translation on a limited computer.' *CACM*, Vol. 2, p. 18, (Nov. 1959).

Knuth, D. E., 'On the translation of languages from left to right.' *Information and Control*, Vol. 8, p. 607. (1965).

Luccio, F., 'A comment on index register allocation.' *CACM*, Vol. 10, p. 572. (1967).

Maurer, W. P., 'An improved hash code for scatter storage', *CACM*, Vol. 11, p. 35. (Jan. 1968).

McClure, R. M., 'TMG—a syntax directed compiler.' *Proceedings ACM National Conference*, p. 262. (1965).

Morris, R., 'Scatter storage techniques', *CACM*, Vol. 11, p. 38. (Jan. 1968).

Nakata, I., 'On compiling algorithms for arithmetic expressions.' *CACM*, Vol. 10, p. 492. (Aug. 1967).

Naur, P. *et al.*, 'Revised report on the algorithmic language Algol 60.' *CACM*, Vol. 6, p. 1. (Jan. 1963).

Northcote, R. S., and Steiner, A. J., 'A syntax loader and subscanner for a compiler-compiler.' *Univ. Illinois Digital Computer Laboratory Report*, No. COO-1018-1031. (1964).

Peterson, W. W., 'Addressing for random-access storage.' *IBM Journal of Research and Development*, Vol. 1, p. 130. (1957).

Plaskow, J., and Schuman, S., 'The TRANGEN system on the M460 computer.' *Computer Associates Inc. Report*. (July 1966).

Pratt, T. W., and Lindsay, R. K., 'A processor-building system for experimental programming languages.' *FJCC*, p. 613. (1966).

Randell, B., and Russell, L. J., 'Algol 60 Implementation.' *Academic Press*. (1964).

Reynolds, J. C., 'An introduction to the COGENT programming system.' *Proceedings ACM National Conference*, p. 422. (1965).

Rosen, S., 'Programming systems and languages,' *McGraw Hill*. (1967).

Ross, D. T., 'A generalised technique for symbol manipulation and numerical calculation.' *CACM*, Vol. 4 p. 147. (March 1961).

Ross, D. T., 'The AED free storage package.' *CACM*, Vol. 10, p. 481. (Aug. 1967).

Ross, D. T., and Rodriguez, J. E., 'Theoretical foundations for the computer-aided design project.' *SJCC* (1963).

Schay, G., and Spruth, W. G., 'Analysis of a file addressing method.' *CACM*, Vol. 5, p. 459. (Aug. 1962).

Schorre, D. V., 'META II, a syntax-oriented compiler writing language.' *Proceedings ACM National Conference*, D1.3. (1964).

Shapiro, R. M., and Zand, L. J., 'A description of the input language for the Compiler Generator System.' *Computer Associates Inc. Report*, No. CA-6306-0112. (June 1963).

Sheridan, P. B., 'The arithmetic translator-compiler of the IBM Fortran automatic coding system.' *CACM*, Vol. 2, p. 9. (Feb. 1959).

Squires, B. E., 'Lexical analysis by a precedence grammar.' *Univ. Illinois Dept. Computer Science Report.* (1966).

Tabory, R., 'Survey and evaluation of AED system at MIT.' *IBM Report,* No. TR 00.1383. (Feb. 1966).

Wegner, P., 'Introduction to systems programming.' *Academic Press.* (1962).

Wirth, N., and Weber, H., 'Euler: a generalisation of Algol, and its formal definition.' *CACM,* Vol. 9, p. 13 (Jan. 1966) and *CACM,* Vol. 9, p. 89. (Feb. 1966).

Zand, L. J., 'A description of the input language for the Compiler Generator System, Vol. 2: MDL.' *Computer Associates Inc. Report,* No. CA-6404-0114. (April 1964).

INDEX

Names of authors are in *italics*

Analysis record, 112
Array, 5, 12
Assembler, 1, 26
Atom, 8
Average length of search, 18

Base address, 8
Bead, 9
Belady algorithm, 96
Binary search, 18
BNF, 31
Bottom-up analysis, 60
Bushed tree, 114

C-structure, 45
Canonical parse, 32
Case pointer, 37
Chomsky classification, 31
Circular list, 8
Code generation, 2, 65
Common sub-expression, 81
Compiler, 1
Composite symbol table, 39
Computed entry table, 19
Context sensitive, 31
Conversion table, 36
Coupling bit, 87

Delay bit, 87
Derived key, 16
Direct access table, 16
Directed graph, 6, 82
Directly produces, 32
Directly reduces, 32
Dope vector, 13

Element, 8
Extendible compiler, 106

Fast-back, 57, 113
Finite state language, 32, 39
Floating point constants, 39
Floyd productions, 54, 114
Folding, 28

Glennie's syntax machine, 42
Global optimisation, 90

Grammar, 31
Graph table, 82

Handle, 33, 46
Hash table, 19, 82

Iliffe vectors, 13
Internal storage structures, 7
Item, 4

Key, 5, 16
Key transformation table, 19

L-language, 36
Leaf, 6
Left corner bottom-up, 62
Left recursive, 34, 111
Length of search, 17
Lexical analysis, 2, 35
LHS back link, 86
Line reconstruction, 37
List, 8
List processing, 9
Loader, 1
Loop, 6
Loop-free, 6

Mapping function, 16, 27
Minimum change branch, 101
Mode transfer function, 75, 78

Name field, 20
Node, 6
Non-terminal symbol, 30

Object code, 4
Occurrence number, 82
Open hash, 20
Operand, 51
Operator, 51
Operator class, 64
Operator grammar, 49
Operator table, 64
Optimisation, 2
Overflow, 20
Overflow hash, 24